# THE WORLD JESUS KNEW

## A CURIOUS KID'S GUIDE TO LIFE IN THE FIRST CENTURY

BY MARC OLSON
ILLUSTRATED BY JEMIMA MAYBANK

beaming books
MINNEAPOLIS

First hardcover edition published 2017 by Sparkhouse Family.
First paperback edition published 2023 by Beaming Books.

28  27  26  25 24 23          2 3 4 5 6 7 8

Hardcover ISBN: 978-1-5064-2500-9
Paperback ISBN: 978-1-5064-5551-8
eBook ISBN: 978-1-5064-2692-1

Written by Marc Olson
Illustrated by Jemima Maybank
Designed by Tory Herman

Library of Congress Control Number: 2022041884

VN0004589; 9781506455518; JAN2023

Beaming Books
PO Box 1209
Minneapolis, MN 55440-1209
Beamingbooks.com

Dedicated to Sigurd and Dane,
my curious, serious, creative, and kind sons,
and to my own patient parents,
who gave me a world to explore and adore.

# TABLE OF CONTENTS

# INTRODUCTION

This is a book about Jesus. Sort of. It's about discovering more about Jesus by exploring the ancient world he lived in. And because we know about the life of Jesus almost exclusively from the Bible, this is also a book about the Bible—especially the part known as the New Testament.

This is a book born from curiosity. Jesus used the things in his world—the plants, the people, the land, the politics, the food—to teach people about God and the ways God works in the world. The people Jesus talked to knew all about these things, the way you know the color of the flowers that grow in your yard or the smell of your favorite meal.

But we live several centuries and many miles away from the world Jesus knew. So what was he talking about? What did the size of a mustard seed or the flavor of salt have to do with anything? Why would Jesus use these things to tell people about life with God?

If you've wondered about that, this is the book for you. Thanks to the rich variety of tools supplied by centuries of scholarship in history, archaeology, and sociology, we're able to explore answers and collect insights about the people and places and things Jesus knew so well.

## Where Are We?

This book focuses on a specific place in the world. Jesus of Nazareth spent the thirty or so years of his life in this region, in places governed by Jewish kings but ruled by the Roman Empire.

This place has been called by various names over the centuries, including Canaan, Palestine, Judea, and Israel. Because it's where Jesus lived and walked and worked, Christians sometimes call it The Holy Land. It's a fairly narrow and long parcel between the Jordan River and the Mediterranean Sea. This area is not wholly part of Africa, Europe, or Asia, so it's often known as the "Middle East." Human beings have lived in this place for more than 10,000 years. The Middle East is often in turmoil because of its religious and historical significance to Christians, Jews, and Muslims.

In this book, we're choosing to call the area Palestine. Historically, that's been the name given to this geographic region between Egypt, Syria, and Arabia. Today, this name is also often used to describe territory owned and occupied by Arab residents of the land, as distinct from the modern state of Israel.

## When Are We?

Jesus lived more than 2,000 years ago. And that's a very long time! The world Jesus knew was in some ways very different from ours, but in other ways—lots of ways—it was the same. People worked, walked, slept, and ate. They had friendships, held parties, told stories, got sick, built stuff, and found ways to dispose of their trash. They used money, wore clothes, played games, and went to school.

**2500 BCE**

The world was already ancient when Jesus was walking around. The Great Pyramid at Giza, along the Nile River in Egypt, was already more than two thousand years old when Jesus was born! As a Jew, Jesus knew thousand-year-old stories of his ancestors. Over in China, people of the Liangzhu culture had been making clothing and fabric out of silk for more than twenty-five centuries.

**Between 7 BCE–6 CE**

Jesus is born.

In putting this book together, we went looking for information. And here's the thing about ancient information: there's not a lot of it. So this book consists of the following:

## WHAT WE KNOW
There are some documented facts about the world Jesus knew. These come from written sources that have survived over the years, including parts of the Bible.

## WHAT WE THINK WE KNOW
Based on these facts and ancient witnesses, we make some assumptions and projections that seem to make sense.

## WHAT WE KNOW WE DON'T KNOW
An awful lot.

## WHAT WE DON'T KNOW WE DON'T KNOW
Probably even more.
Our vision of Jesus' time will always be incomplete. But we can study and imagine his life, knowing that it has plenty to tell us about our own.

## But be warned.
This book may very well change the way you read, understand, experience, and even feel about the Bible and the stories it contains. Just as a magnifying glass can transform a backyard or strip of city woods into a strange and fascinating new world, so also the windows and lenses and looks suggested here can help you see the old, old Bible in some new and exciting ways. And that closer look might make you think more about how to live as a follower of Jesus in the world you know. Are you ready?

A. The Mediterranean is the earth's largest sea (based on surface area). It connects to the Atlantic Ocean. The name *Mediterranean* means "middle of the earth."

B. The Mediterranean coastline is about 180 miles long.

C. The city of Bethlehem is 5,696 miles from New York City.

D. The city of Jerusalem sits at almost the same latitude as San Diego. It is 2,474 feet above sea level.

E. Jericho is about 1,000 feet below sea level. Travelers walking to Jerusalem from Jericho would climb 3,300 feet!

F. The Jordan is the river with the lowest elevation in the world. It runs about 150 miles.

G. The surface of the Dead Sea is Earth's lowest elevation on land (1,388 feet below sea level).

H. In the Bible, the Dead Sea is called the Salt Sea, the Sea of the Arabah, and the Eastern Sea (but never the Dead Sea). It's actually a lake, and it's 8.6 times saltier than the ocean.

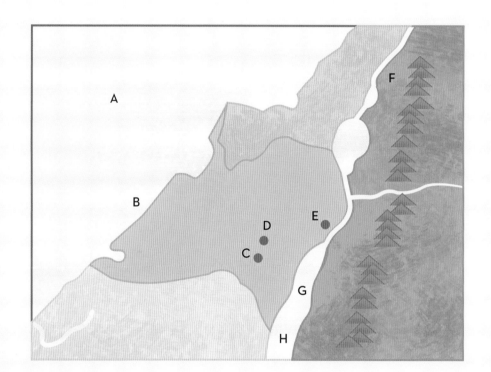

**476 CE**

Rome falls.

**1163**

The Notre Dame Cathedral is built.

**1215**

The Magna Carta is written.

**1601**

Shakespeare writes *Hamlet*.

**1861**

The US Civil War starts.

**1969**

Neil Armstrong walks on the moon.

# THE STRUCTURE OF SOCIETY

Every society has some sort of structure, an unspoken set of rules about how that society functions. Who's in charge? Who gets what from whom? How do people live together in a way that makes sense? In Jesus' time, the answers were very clear: one group of people got a lot, and everyone else had to help them get it.

First-century Palestine was a place of huge inequalities when it came to things like power and wealth. So think of the social structure like a pyramid, with a few groups of people at the tiny top who enjoy the benefits of the work done by the many groups of people at the bottom.

• • • • • • • • • • •

Wealth and power moved from the bottom to the top of the pyramid—the higher you were, the more of both you had. And the people in the middle were stuck squabbling about who was more important in an effort to grab a little of each as they clawed their way up.

Most of the people who lived in Jesus' time were very poor and had very little power (we'll call them peasants and slaves), while a few were very wealthy and had the power to make decisions that affected everybody else (we'll refer to them as elites). The peasants and slaves worked hard, growing and tending crops, fishing, or herding animals. The elites, who owned and controlled the land and lakes, did not work themselves but earned money from the work of the peasants by charging them taxes, rents, and tributes. In between the elites and the peasants and slaves were people who collected taxes, as well as a class of artisans who had special skills like stone cutting, weaving, and pottery.

• • • • • • • • • • •

This social structure was in place no matter where someone lived. Cities, like Caesarea and Tiberias, were built under the direction of rulers as a way of getting favors from the emperors for whom they named the cities. The labor and wealth of the countryside was exploited (used to an unfair extent) to build and maintain cities and to supply all the needs (and wants) of the elites who lived in them.

Rural areas were divided into big estates and owned mostly by city dwellers. They were operated by peasants and slaves.

## THE ROMAN EMPEROR

This guy (it was always a man) held all the power—and shared or gave it away only when it suited his interests.

## RULERS

King Herod, Herod Antipas, Herod Philip, Pilate

## ELITES

Soldiers, Priests, Land Owners, Tax Collectors

Jesus' ministry touched and troubled these groups most of all.

## PEASANTS

Artisans, Farmers, Fishers, Herders, Workers

## SLAVES

Household Slaves, Day Laborers

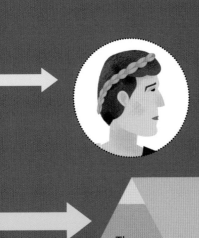

These families made alliances and deals with each other.

These families competed for friendship and recognition from the rulers. They controlled most of the land, fishing rights, and ways of getting crops to market. Their wealth came from the work of the peasants.

Wealth from produce and labor

Favors, gifts, protection

Loyalty, tributes

These folks recognized they had a pretty bad deal. They worked on land they didn't own, they didn't get to keep most of what they harvested or herded, and on top of that—they had to pay rent! They paid the taxes that they had to but also looked for ways to cheat the system.

Jesus came from this part of society. Our best guess is that 85-90 percent of the population of Palestine at the time of Jesus was part of the peasant class and worked at farming, fishing, and herding, as well as processing grain, fruit, fish, meat, and wool.

Slaves and day laborers were so deep in debt that they had to work for others without getting paid. These people owned very little.

Denarius
(silver coin)

Areus
(gold coin)

Sestertius
(brass coin)

# CURRENCY

Grapes for wine

Olive oil

Wheat

In this system, you could move sideways or down, but you never moved up to a new level.

# WHAT GROWS HERE?

Because of where it sits on the planet—between the arid deserts of Egypt and North Africa and the more humid, not-quite-tropical areas of the eastern Mediterranean—the land of Palestine enjoys a good climate for growing all kinds of plants and trees. Winters are wet and mild, and temperatures don't often fall below freezing. Summers are hot and dry, especially in the low-elevation desert.

Only a few rivers flow all year round. The Jordan River is fed in the spring and summer by melting snow from Mount Hermon. Rainfall decreases as you travel east and south. In the southern Negeb Desert, some years see no rain at all!

## BECAUSE THERE IS SO MUCH VARIETY IN THE ELEVATION AND PHYSICAL GEOGRAPHY OF THIS AREA, JUST ABOUT ANYTHING CAN GROW HERE.

Mustard Plant

Mustard Seeds

Pomegranate

The name *pomegranate* comes from ancient words that mean "many-seeded apple." When the Bible mentions apples, it could be talking about pomegranates.

Cyclamen

Lilies

Lupine

Anemone

### Food

In the book of Deuteronomy, God describes what the people will find when they come to live in the land. That list (Deut. 8:8) includes wheat and barley, figs, grapes, olives, pomegranates, and honey. These have remained important food sources in the area for thousands of years.

### Flowers

Not long after the first winter rains fall in October and November, the land turns green and blossoms until the next dry season.

Pink and white cyclamen and red, white, and purple anemones bloom from December into March. Next come the blue lupine and yellow corn marigold.

Marigold

Flax

Fig Tree

Figs

Wheat

Barley

Crocus

Several native plants, including the crocus, are called geophytes (geo- = "earth") because they store nourishment in their bulbs underground.

Cypress Tree

Terebinth Tree

Olive Tree

Date Palm

Olives

Mount Tabor Oak

Grapevine

Willow Tree

Carob Tree

## Trees

The land along the coast enjoys a mild Mediterranean climate. Low shrubs and grasses grow here, along with Mount Tabor oaks along the hills.

The steppes and desert areas of the east and south are so dry and hot that only the hardiest plants can survive, including the date palm, which will tolerate even salty and brackish oasis water.

Common oak and plane trees, as well as terebinth and carob trees, grow at higher elevations and in the northern part of the land.

# THE JEWISH PEOPLE

### God's Chosen People

Jesus was Jewish. He grew up following the traditions and rules of the Jewish people. So if we want to know about Jesus, we need to know about this very important part of his life and culture. Being Jewish is more than

## PEOPLE WITH A TEMPLE

The Jerusalem Temple was built by King Solomon about 1,000 years before Jesus was born. It was destroyed in 587 BCE and partially rebuilt in 515 BCE. During Jesus' time, it was being rebuilt and enlarged. This temple was the place where Jews offered sacrifices to God. It was the center of religious life. Sacrifices were made by temple priests, and a powerful High Priest presided over it all. In addition to offering sacrifices and tithes at the temple, every Jew paid a temple tax each year. The temple was a pilgrimage destination. All Jewish males over twelve years old had to journey to Jerusalem three times a year for the festivals of Passover, Pentecost, and Sukkoth. Often, whole families made these trips.

## PEOPLE OF THE BOOK

Perhaps even more important than the temple was the Torah, or Hebrew scriptures. The scriptures told the history of the Jewish people and the God who chose them to bless the world. The Torah also contained all of the teachings and laws that explained how God wanted God's people to live. The study and teaching of the Torah was a huge part of Jewish life in Jesus' time (and it still is). Much of this happened in synagogues and other gathering places in villages and cities all across the land. Torah teachers were called rabbis. A *synagogue* is both a gathering of people and a gathering place for worship, Torah study, teaching, and community life.

## PEOPLE WHO DIDN'T ALWAYS GET ALONG

Even though they shared the same scriptures, customs, and family history, not all Jews in Jesus' time thought or worshipped or acted the same. Different groups had different opinions and wanted different things. And they didn't always get along. There are a few groups we know about:

### Sadducees
- Members of upper-class Jerusalem families
- Served as priests and judges
- Obeyed Torah laws, especially laws about worship in the temple
- Didn't believe in angels, demons, or the resurrection from the dead

### Essenes
- Followed strict religious purity laws
- Were critics of the temple leadership and worship
- Lived apart from other communities

### Pharisees
- Not priests, and not from priestly families
- Torah scholars and rabbis
- Taught, interpreted, and argued about the scriptures
- Known for careful, pious, and holy living according to the laws of the Torah

### Zealots
- A political movement; wanted to free the Jews from Roman occupation
- Came from many classes of society
- Were willing to be violent to achieve their goals

### Regular people
Most Jews in Jesus' time didn't really fall into any of these categories. They lived regular lives. They worked hard, tried to follow the commandments, observed the customs of their faith, married, had babies, lived, and died.

simply belonging to a religious group. The Jewish people—in the Old Testament, they're called the Israelites or Hebrews—are an ancient and ongoing family who believe they are set apart by God. This family traces its roots all the way back to ancestral parents we read about in the Old Testament—also known as the Hebrew Bible—people like Abraham and Sarah, Joseph, Noah, Ruth, Esther, David, and so many more. As members of this family, Jews today understand God's ancient promises and covenants as promises to and covenants with *them and their children* as well.

## PEOPLE WHO RESTED

The seven-day Jewish week begins on what we now know as Sunday and ends with a big celebration of the seventh day, called Shabbat, meaning "Sabbath." The word *Shabbat* comes from the Hebrew root that means "cease, end, or rest." In ancient Israel, the Sabbath was the only day with a name—all the rest were just known by number. The Sabbath was a gift and a commandment (see Exodus 31:15-17).

For Jewish people, the Sabbath day was—and is—a weekly ritual and one of the most important parts of their religious identity. People observed the Sabbath commandment by celebrating with family and by refraining from work. We don't have a perfect list of all the activities that weren't allowed on the Sabbath in Jesus' time (he, the Pharisees, and the Sadducees argued about these things). Later lists included thirty-nine activities that were off limits, including:

- Sowing (planting)
- Plowing
- Reaping (harvesting)
- Binding sheaves of grain
- Grinding
- Kneading dough
- Baking or cooking
- Shearing wool
- Washing clothes
- Sewing or weaving
- Building
- Demolishing
- Writing more than two letters
- Making a fire
- Putting out a fire
- Butchering
- Tying a knot

There was agreement that any of these things *could* be done on the Sabbath in order to save a life. Jesus got in trouble with some of the religious authorities for healing people and for picking grain to eat on the Sabbath.

The hard-driving Greeks and Romans thought the Jews were lazy because they took a festival day off from working every week. In the ancient world, rest and leisure time were privileges normally enjoyed only by the very rich.

Just like the seven days described in Genesis 1, Jewish days begin and end at sunset. The Sabbath fell between Jesus' death and his resurrection. In order to avoid working on the Sabbath, Jesus' Jewish friends asked for his body so they could bury him before the Sabbath started at sunset. And the women waited until daybreak of the day following the Sabbath before going to the tomb to care for Jesus' body. Because that was the day—the first day of the week—when the women discovered Jesus had been raised from the dead, Christians call the first day—our modern-day Sunday—"Sabbath."

## PEOPLE HOPING FOR A MESSIAH

The Jews of Jesus' time were being ruled in their own land by the Roman Empire, with foreign soldiers in the streets and non-Jewish laws and customs everywhere. They had to pay taxes to the empire and even make sacrifices to the emperor. This kind of thing had gone on for hundreds of years with very few breaks. Many Jews were looking for and hoping for a powerful Jewish king to rise up, save them, and make things right again. The followers of Jesus believed he was this Messiah. *Messiah* means "anointed, or chosen, one."

# ROMAN RULES

By the time of Jesus, the Roman Empire stretched from the northern coast of what is now France all the way south to Egypt and east to Armenia. In order to control such a huge and far-flung empire, Rome's rulers relied on local kings to provide order and control and to make sure goods and money kept flowing back to Rome.

In Palestine, Herod the Great was such a king. He worked hard to remain on the emperor's good side *and* stay popular enough with the people of Judea, Samaria, and Galilee to avoid all-out revolution. Herod was a shrewd operator and a good builder. His renovation of the Jerusalem Temple, which he made into a magnificent structure, raised his status in the empire while helping to keep the Jews tolerant of Rome's rule.

## Emperor

## Herod

## HOW IT WORKS

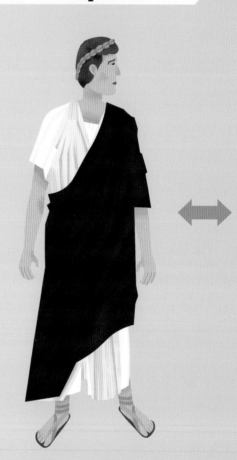

The emperor gives the role of "king" to someone like Herod.

Herod is king and now owes the emperor loyalty, support, and money.

### Herod, Herod, or Herod? (Lots of kings with the same name.)

It's easy to get confused with all the Herods mentioned in the Bible. Are they the same person? What's going on here? The name *Herod* is kind of like a family last name. Herod the Great was given the kingship of the whole region in the year 37 BCE by the Roman emperor Octavian Augustus. He was king and had lots of power in Palestine and the surrounding territory but was a client-king, which means he owed the emperor for his position and did what the emperor wanted him to do.

Herod the Great ruled this area until he died in 4 BCE. After that, the kingdom got split up, and rule was shared by three of his sons. Herod Antipas ruled the regions of Galilee and Perea. Herod Philip ruled the northern territories of Iturea, Gaulanitis, Trachonitis, Batanea, and Aurantis. Herod Archelaus tried to rule Judea, Samaria, and Idumea, but he was a pretty rotten king and was exiled after only a few years. Between them, they ruled the region.

The politics and economy of Palestine had been part of the Roman Empire for nearly one hundred years when Jesus started his ministry. Jesus, his disciples, and the many people who followed him faced the facts of life under the empire every day. They were expected to pay taxes and tolls, had to make way for Roman soldiers in their streets, and watched big, foreign-looking cities spring up to honor distant, toga-clad nobles they would never meet.

Because Jesus and prophets like John the Baptist were popular enough to have many followers, they posed a threat to the power structures set up by Rome's rulers.

## Patrons

Herod picks powerful families to help him rule. In exchange, they owe him loyalty, support, and money. This type of setup is known as a patron-client relationship. When things go wrong, people with more power fix it by replacing the people with less power. People with no power get used, and often abused.

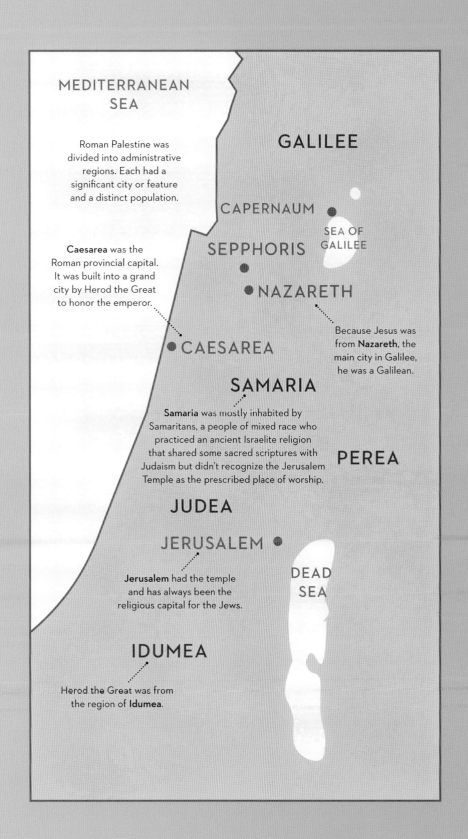

**MEDITERRANEAN SEA**

Roman Palestine was divided into administrative regions. Each had a significant city or feature and a distinct population.

**Caesarea** was the Roman provincial capital. It was built into a grand city by Herod the Great to honor the emperor.

**GALILEE**

**CAPERNAUM** ●

SEA OF GALILEE

**SEPPHORIS**

● **NAZARETH**

Because Jesus was from **Nazareth**, the main city in Galilee, he was a Galilean.

● **CAESAREA**

**SAMARIA**

**Samaria** was mostly inhabited by Samaritans, a people of mixed race who practiced an ancient Israelite religion that shared some sacred scriptures with Judaism but didn't recognize the Jerusalem Temple as the prescribed place of worship.

**PEREA**

**JUDEA**

**JERUSALEM** ●

**Jerusalem** had the temple and has always been the religious capital for the Jews.

**DEAD SEA**

**IDUMEA**

Herod the Great was from the region of **Idumea**.

# THE ROMAN ARMY

The Romans were really good at being an empire. They built great roads, figured out how to bring fresh water into cities, and had an amazing and scary army. The Roman military was disciplined, dangerous, and impressive. They had the swords and knew how to use them. From the time General Pompey conquered the region in 63 BCE until the Romans destroyed the Jerusalem Temple in 70 CE, the Roman military was visible throughout Palestine. Jesus' whole life was spent in the presence of an occupying army.

## Auxiliaries

Once an area became part of the empire, the Roman army recruited local people to serve as soldiers. Non-citizens couldn't become legionaries (below), but they could be part of the army as auxiliaries. Auxiliaries were trained in the Roman way and got some equipment. They were paid less than normal soldiers but could become citizens if they survived to retirement.

## A Legionary
### 1

The Roman infantry soldier. He was usually a Roman citizen and signed up for twenty-five years of service. He was provided all his weapons, armor, and gear, and was paid 255 silver denarii , basically a starting salary, each year.

## A Contubernia
### 8

Made up of eight soldiers. These eight guys did everything together.

**1 contubernia = 8 legionaries**
Soldiers ate together, made camp, hauled water, gathered firewood, and fought beside each other.

## A Century
### 80

Made up of around 80 soldiers (despite the name).

**1 century = 10 contuberniae**
Each century was commanded by an officer, called a centurion, and his assistant, called the optio.

## A Cohort
### 500

Made up of around 500 soldiers. The first cohort in each legion was special, and had around 1,000 members.

**1 cohort = 6 centuries**
Senior centurions commanded cohorts.

## A Legion
### 5000

Made up of around 5,000 soldiers, plus supporting troops (called auxiliaries) and cavalry (soldiers on horseback).

**1 legion = 10 cohorts**
Each legion had a special commanding officer, called the legate.

During the time of Jesus, Rome had up to thirty legions deployed throughout the empire (more than 150,000 fighting men). In Palestine, several cohorts of auxiliary troops kept the peace, served as police, and reminded everybody who was in charge.

# A ROMAN CENTURION

The Roman army developed a reputation for producing professional soldiers who knew about building, diplomacy, and government, as well as fighting. Centurions were commanding officers. They were Roman citizens who made careers as tough soldiers who led by example. Centurions trained troops and commanded groups of eighty soldiers (a century). Centurions brought the powerful presence of the empire wherever they went.

In Palestine, senior centurions commanded 1,000 or so auxiliaries—soldiers who were recruited from Syria and Samaria. Centurions taught them how to be soldiers and enforced the rules of Roman military life—which sometimes included beating them with a cane made of vine wood.

Centurions in Judea were part of the elite class and often had families who lived with them. They were paid fifteen times what a regular soldier earned in a year. They were a big deal.

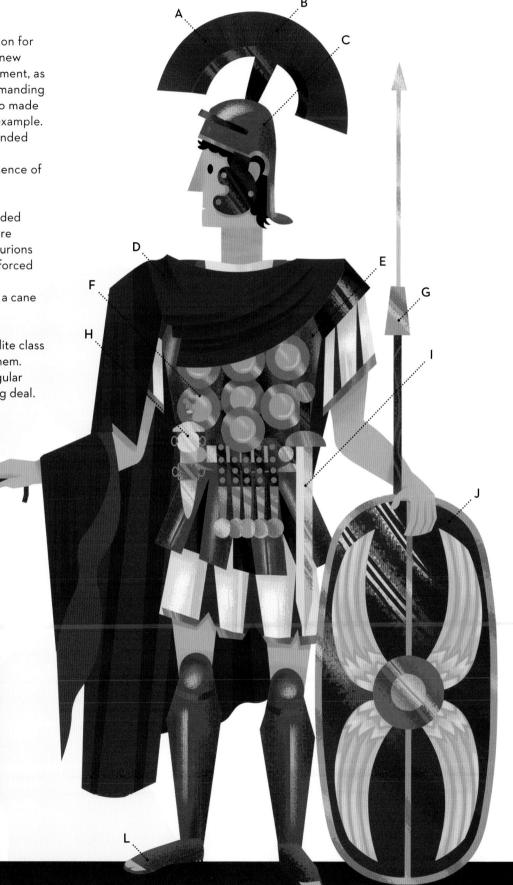

A.  Dyed horsehair
B.  Sideways horsehair crest on helmet
C.  Helmet
D.  A cloak of fine cloth
E.  Leather or metal breastplate
F.  Medals for bravery in battle
G.  Pila
H.  Dagger on right side
I.  Gladius/sword on left side
J.  Scutum
K.  Wooden vine wood cane used to beat subordinates
L.  Spiked caligae for marching

# CRIME AND PUNISHMENT

## Roman Laws

These laws were administered by the governor or prefect of the Roman province of Judea. This person had the power of life and death over every person in the province. Major cases, like murder or insurrection, were heard by the prefect. More minor cases were heard by magistrates appointed by the prefect. Pontius Pilate was prefect of Judea from 26 to 36 CE.

### Crime

**Minor**
- Theft
- Fraud

**Major**
- Robbery
- Arson
- Murder
- Rioting
- Stealing from the temple
- Insurrection or treason

### Punishment

Prison wasn't used as punishment in the ancient world, but as a place to put people who were awaiting trial or sentencing. In general, the more serious the crime, the more serious the punishment. Among the Romans, most punishments were harsh, and included:
- Fines
- Enslavement
- Beating or whipping
- Execution
- Exile

The Romans used a **scourge**, or whip, to beat convicts. It was called a **flagellum**, and had lead weights on the ends of leather straps. Romans would also beat criminals with a bundle of birch rods.

Any crime committed by a slave could end in execution. Slaves had very few legal rights. Sometimes, if one slave in a household was convicted of a crime, all of the slaves in the house were executed!

The Latin word for prison or prison cell is *carcer*. We get the word **incarceration** directly from the Romans.

ONLY ROME CAN PUNISH ME

A Roman citizen was exempt from local judgment. They could only be tried by Roman courts, and usually got off by paying fines.

## Jewish Laws

Jewish religious laws generally didn't interest the Romans. Jewish laws were administered by Jewish religious courts. They imposed religious penalties, including **excommunication** from—which means getting kicked out of—the synagogue. They could also charge fines or administer beatings or lashings. Jewish-law crimes were things like breaking the Sabbath by working, violating the temple, blasphemy against God, and adultery. Jewish punishment was usually intended to restore broken community trust.

\* **Jesus lived under two kinds of law—Roman law and Jewish law.**
Jesus was accused of **blasphemy** (insulting or speaking disrespectfully about God) by the Jewish court, and **insurrection** (rebelling against the government) under Roman law. He was sentenced to death by **crucifixion**. Crucifixion was a method of execution reserved for the worst criminals.

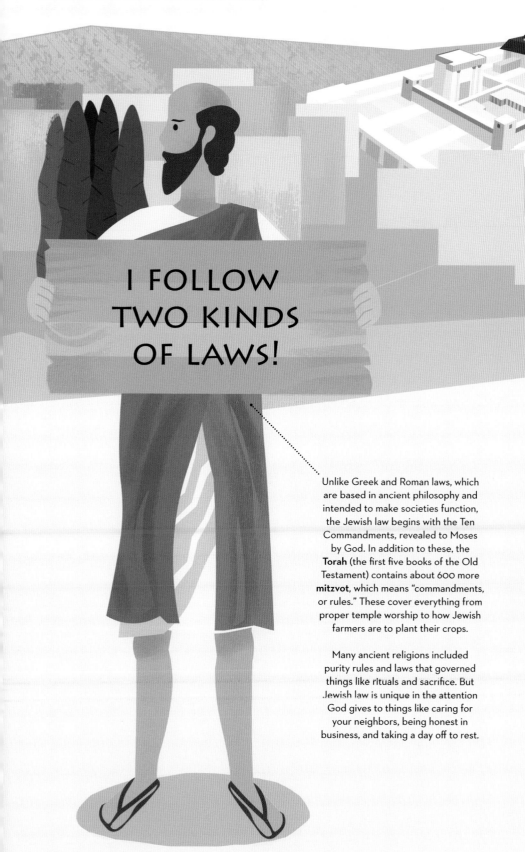

I FOLLOW TWO KINDS OF LAWS!

Unlike Greek and Roman laws, which are based in ancient philosophy and intended to make societies function, the Jewish law begins with the Ten Commandments, revealed to Moses by God. In addition to these, the **Torah** (the first five books of the Old Testament) contains about 600 more **mitzvot**, which means "commandments, or rules." These cover everything from proper temple worship to how Jewish farmers are to plant their crops.

Many ancient religions included purity rules and laws that governed things like rituals and sacrifice. But Jewish law is unique in the attention God gives to things like caring for your neighbors, being honest in business, and taking a day off to rest.

### Crime
- Sacrificing your child to the god Moloch
- Practicing divination (speaking with spirits)
- Luring people to idolatry
- Breaking the Sabbath
- Prophesying in the name of a false god
- Adultery
- Being rude to your father or mother (check it out: Deuteronomy 21:18-21)

### Punishment
Not all laws had specific punishments, so policing law-breakers was often more a matter of arguing about interpretation and application, as well as a matter of public shaming. The Sanhedrin (Jewish law court) would make judgments on matters of law and prescribe consequences.

Some crimes against Jewish law carried stiff penalties, including fines, flogging, and even death. Death by stoning was practiced in Jesus' time too.

The book of Leviticus is all about the Jewish law, and was meant to help Jewish people know how to live well with God, the earth, and each other. Take a look at these laws from chapter 19:
- Do not go over your vineyard a second time or pick up the grapes that have fallen. Leave them for the poor and the foreigner (verse 10).
- Do not hold back the wages of a hired worker overnight (verse 13).
- Do not seek revenge or bear a grudge against anyone among your people, but love your neighbor as yourself (verse 18).
- Do not plant your field with two kinds of seed (verse 19).
- Stand up in the presence of the aged, show respect for the elderly and revere your God (verse 32).
- When a foreigner resides among you in your land, do not mistreat them (verse 33).

Because it touched on so many aspects of ordinary life, following God's law was a significant part of a Jewish person's daily doings, and a frequent topic of conversation, teaching, and argument. This close connection between faith and the details of life kept Jewish people thinking about God all day long.

# GETTING AROUND

Land travel in ancient Palestine was always by foot. If you were a regular person, you hoofed it on your own two feet. If you had the means, you got to use the power and energy supplied by other people or animals.

Mostly people walked. They used paths between homes within villages, and trails and paths between towns. There was usually more than one way to get somewhere. Well-worn roads between cities and larger towns linked to the impressive, paved Roman road system. A walking person leading a loaded donkey could go about three miles an hour and cover about twenty-three miles in a day.

People traveled to visit relatives, to sell and buy goods that weren't available locally, and to participate in religious holidays and festivals. Jews celebrated three pilgrimage festivals during the year, in which families traveled from their homes throughout the land to the Holy City of Jerusalem and its temple. These three festivals—**Passover**, **Shavuot**, and **Sukkoth**—required the faithful to journey to Jerusalem and stay there for the length of the festival, usually a few days. Often whole villages of people traveled to these festivals together.

**Horses:** Most of the horses in the time of Jesus were used for military or government purposes. Rumor has it King Herod the Great had six thousand horses in his cavalry. Official messengers on horseback, using the Roman roads and switching horses at intervals, could travel hundreds of miles in just a few days.

**Litters**: Among the Romans and wannabe-Romans, a special kind of bed called a litter was used to carry imperial dignitaries and very wealthy people. These required two or more slaves to carry them. Litters were most commonly used in cities and towns, and not for long-distance travel.

Chariots: Chariots were usually pulled by horses. They were weapons of war, but also got used from time to time to transport officials. One New Testament story has Philip hitching a ride on a chariot with the court treasurer of the kingdom of Ethiopia. They were probably traveling on a mostly smooth Roman road.

Camels: Camels could carry riders, and endure dryness and heat. They also spit, bit, and were usually even slower than walking. Camels were very good long-distance cargo haulers. And did we mention the spitting?

Donkeys: Donkeys could carry heavy loads, pull plows or carts, and, in a pinch, be ridden by people. They were slower than horses, but sure-footed on steep climbs over the mountains.

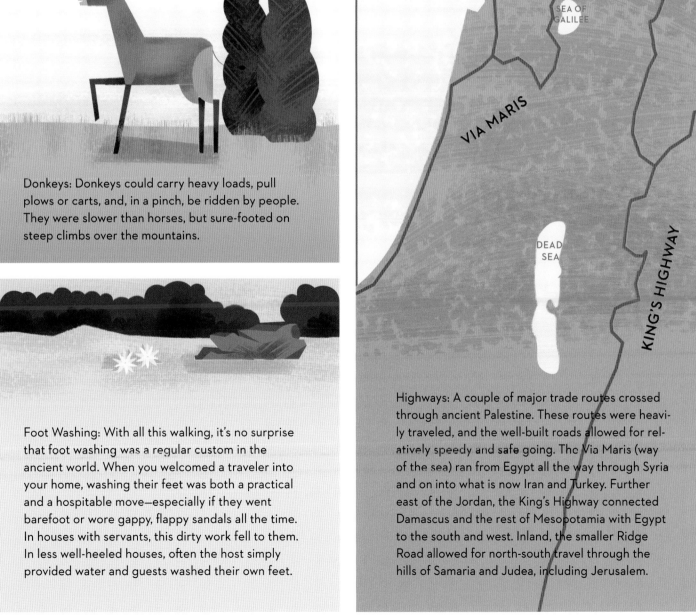

Foot Washing: With all this walking, it's no surprise that foot washing was a regular custom in the ancient world. When you welcomed a traveler into your home, washing their feet was both a practical and a hospitable move—especially if they went barefoot or wore gappy, flappy sandals all the time. In houses with servants, this dirty work fell to them. In less well-heeled houses, often the host simply provided water and guests washed their own feet.

Highways: A couple of major trade routes crossed through ancient Palestine. These routes were heavily traveled, and the well-built roads allowed for relatively speedy and safe going. The Via Maris (way of the sea) ran from Egypt all the way through Syria and on into what is now Iran and Turkey. Further east of the Jordan, the King's Highway connected Damascus and the rest of Mesopotamia with Egypt to the south and west. Inland, the smaller Ridge Road allowed for north-south travel through the hills of Samaria and Judea, including Jerusalem.

# ANATOMY OF A ROMAN ROAD

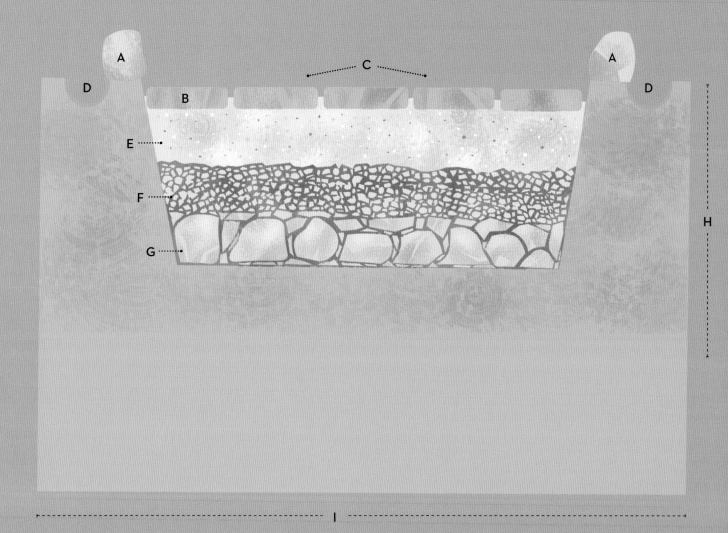

A. Curb stone
B. Large, smooth stone slabs
C. Slightly higher here
D. Drainage gutter
E. Gravel and sand tamped down

F. Smaller stones with added concrete*
G. Large stones, fitted tightly together

H. About 3 feet deep
I. 10–50 feet wide—the more important the road, the wider

\* Romans developed a kind of concrete using volcanic ash and limestone.

# Distances between Jerusalem and . . .

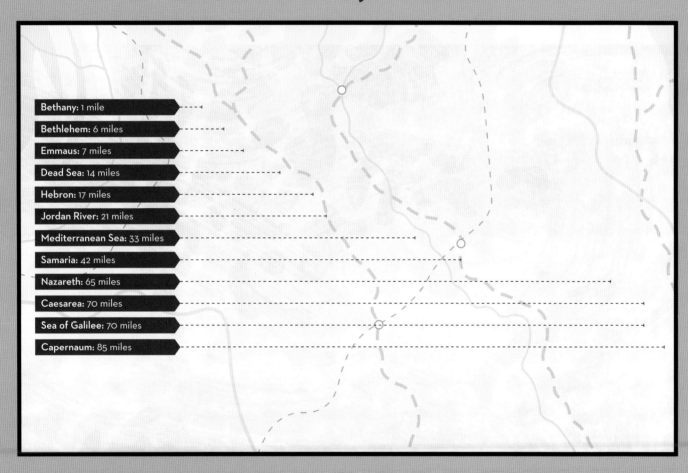

Bethany: 1 mile

Bethlehem: 6 miles

Emmaus: 7 miles

Dead Sea: 14 miles

Hebron: 17 miles

Jordan River: 21 miles

Mediterranean Sea: 33 miles

Samaria: 42 miles

Nazareth: 65 miles

Caesarea: 70 miles

Sea of Galilee: 70 miles

Capernaum: 85 miles

Because Jerusalem sits 2,474 feet above sea level on a ridge of mountains in the middle of the country, it seems like every road to the Holy City requires going uphill. Those traveling the Ridge Road from Galilee and Samaria had less of a climb. If you were coming up from Jericho, though, you would have climbed 3,300 feet over about 20 miles.

The Bible calls the route from Jericho up to Jerusalem the ascent of *Adum'min*, which means the "red ascent." After a rainy journey, guess what color the mud on your feet was?

# HOME LIFE

The word house gets used in the Bible to talk about buildings and dwellings—everything from family homes and compounds all the way up to palaces and the Jerusalem temple, which is called the house of God. The word also gets used to describe families, clans, households, and family trees, as in "the house of David." Most households of regular people included several generations of a family. There needed to be space for everybody, so houses were built to be expanded, or added onto, as the family grew.

## Building a House

Small houses were sometimes built into existing caves. The underground room would stay cool in summer and warm in winter.

Stone was the most common building material. Cut stone required a skilled stonemason with iron tools. Poor people piled uncut rocks to make walls.

Wooden boards were rare and valuable. The wealthy imported cedar from Syria.

Sticks and poles, tied with rope and stuck together with mud, helped keep out wind and rain.

Where stone was scarce, people made sun-dried bricks from mud and straw. Walls made from these bricks had to be repaired frequently.

Tarps and blankets made of rough wool were used for canopies and tents, and could divide rooms too. Nomads, called Bedouin, herded sheep and goats. They lived in tents made from their animals' wool and hair.

In the ancient world, people lived together, and there wasn't much privacy in the way we think of it today. Because of the moderate climate, many of life's activities could happen outdoors, on the rooftops or in courtyards.

Poor families with livestock would share part of their house with the animals.

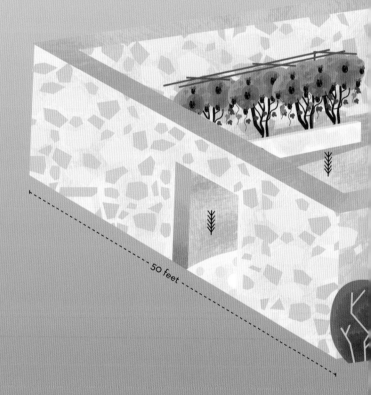

50 feet

The walls of a house like this were made from a dark, local stone called basalt. Poorer families had smaller houses built of less expensive (and less durable) materials. The very rich had houses with tiled roofs, piped water, under-floor heat, and slaves to do the housework. Only the wealthiest people had indoor kitchens. This is an example of a house owned by a well-to-do fishing family in Galilee.

Unlike this family compound, most homes in the cities and towns of Palestine didn't have private, walled courtyards. Often, neighbors shared common outdoor space. Houses opened onto small squares where people cooked, hung laundry to dry, and visited with each other. These were also spaces to do business and make public announcements.

A lot went on "upstairs." Most dwellings utilized the roof space for working, cooking and eating, resting or sleeping, or even bathing. On hot days and nights, sometimes a perch on the roof helped you catch a little breeze. Only the houses of the wealthy had indoor stairs.

Upper room / rooftop

Living areas

Windows were small and few, to help regulate the temperature inside and for security.

Courtyard

Kitchen / cooking area

Walls were made of stone. Roofs were usually made of poles covered by mud and smoothed.

## The *Bet Av*, or "House of the Father"

To understand the shape of the society in Jesus' time, it's important to understand the way the most basic part of that society worked. In ancient Palestine, the smallest part of society wasn't the individual person, but the family. First-century families were shaped like pyramids. There was one ruler at the top (in Jesus' time, this was the father, or **patriarch**). The patriarch was the head of the household. After a son married, he brought his wife into the family home, where they lived with his father and mother. When a daughter was married, she moved into her husband's household.

Under the patriarch in the family pyramid, other members would have status and responsibility in descending order, all the way down to the youngest child. Wealth and honor went up the pyramid, where the father used it, spent it, or gave it away based on what he thought was best for the family. As patriarch of the family, the father protected the less powerful members, who owed him loyalty and obedience.

# GETTING DRESSED

In Jesus' day, everyone, everywhere, wore basically the same outfit. It might vary a bit by your status or gender, but nearly everyone wore some version of a simple tunic, covered by a cloak.

The hem of the tunic went to mid-calf on men, and all the way to women's ankles. Working men sometimes wore a short tunic that only went to mid-thigh.

Sometimes the sides were sewn too, leaving holes for the arms.

The wool or linen undergarment, or tunic, was made like a poncho, with a hole for the head. It was usually belted at the waist.

Sandals were made of wood and/or camel hide and secured to the feet with leather thongs or straps.

Belt, or girdle, of leather or linen.

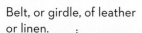

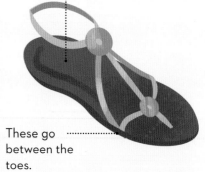

These go between the toes.

## It's All about the Money
Everybody pretty much wore the same basic garments, but these clothes could be very different, depending on the wealth of the wearer. Clothes were a way to show your status.

**Poor People**
- Rough, woven fabric, usually made of sheep wool or goat hair
- No dye; clothes were gray or brown
- No changes of clothes

**Wealthy People**
- Finely spun fabrics, like linen
- All kinds of colors from expensive dyes
- Changes of clothing
- Jewelry

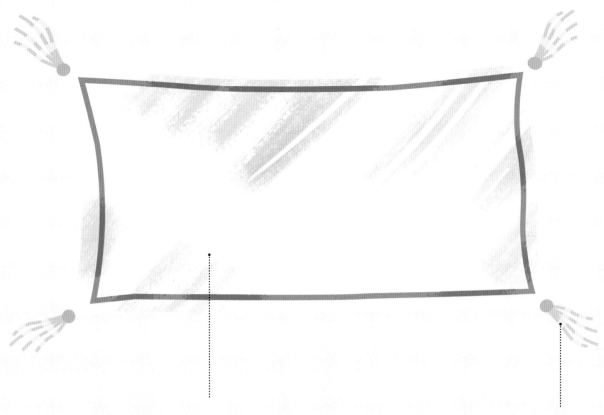

The mantle or cloak, also called a pallium by the Romans, was an outer garment that wrapped around the body or over one or both shoulders. It could also double as a blanket or kind of sleeping bag.

The tassels on men's outer garments were required by the Torah, and reminded the wearer to obey the commandments.

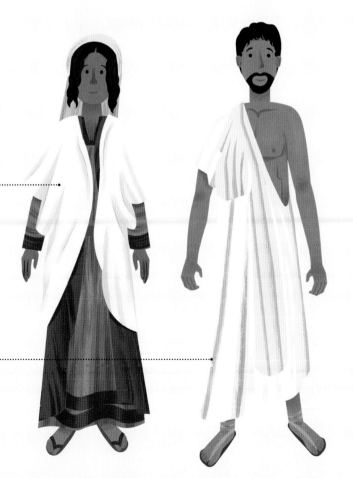

Jewish women wore longer clothes that covered more of their bodies.

Only Roman citizens were allowed to wear the toga.

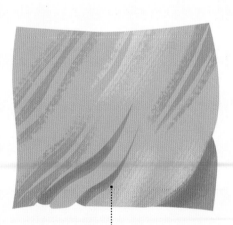

In Jesus' time, Jewish teachers wore head coverings. Other men weren't required to cover their heads, but they sometimes did to keep off the hot sun. For women, head coverings were about modesty, not the weather. Most Roman women—and all Jewish women—would have worn a veil and a shawl-type covering over their hair while outdoors or in public.

## Shoes, Sandals, Boots, and Slippers

Though the ancient Greeks had a victory goddess named Nike, and the biggest river in Palestine was the Jordan, nobody in the first century would have been able to imagine present-day sneakers. Ancient footwear ran the gamut from home-grown calluses on bare feet to the gnarly hobnailed protective boots worn by Roman soldiers. In between these two ends of the spectrum were various types of sandals, closed shoes, and even slippers.

In addition to protecting your toes, and making long walks less painful, what you wore on your feet (or didn't) showed people your status. Roman citizens wouldn't dream of going barefoot; men wouldn't even wear sandals outdoors. To be barefoot suggested you were either a slave or very poor. Among the Jews, being barefoot suggested poverty or voluntary humility. In the Bible, removing one's shoes could be an act of reverence, or a sign of mourning.

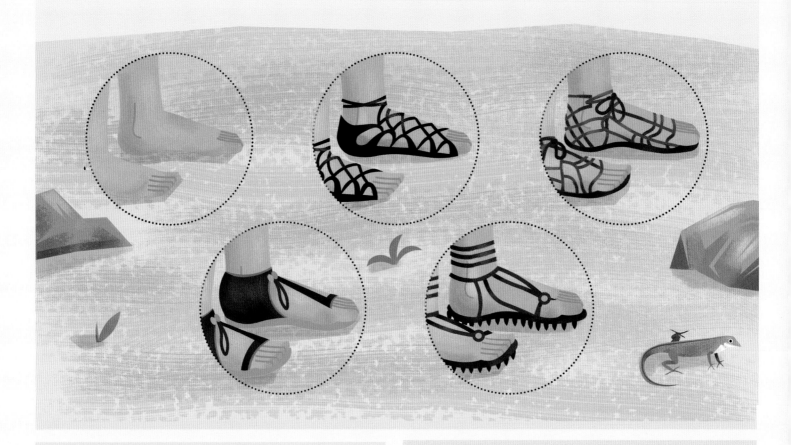

## Bible Rules for Wearers

The Hebrew Bible Jesus would have known—Christians call it the Old Testament—has lots of rules about clothing and jewelry. Jewish people knew these laws and tried to follow them. For example:
Deuteronomy 22:11: Don't wear garments made of mixed fabric.

Numbers 15:38: Always wear tassels to remind you of God's commandments.

(The Bible is silent on the matter of washing clothes in pee.)

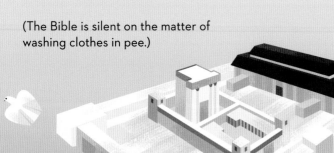

## Slaves

Slaves wore whatever their owners allowed. Some slaves were dressed elegantly, while others wore rags or hand-me-down tunics. Some slaves were made to wear metal collars that indicated the promise of a reward to the person who captured and returned them to their master.

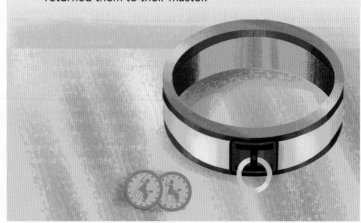

## Roman Ranks and Toga Types

Stripes on a tunic indicated rank:

- Basic = undyed wool, no stripes
- Equestrian class = narrow stripe
- Senatorial class = wide stripe Toga colors mattered too:
- Off-white, undyed wool = Roman citizen (men only)

- Purple border = magistrate or judge
- Black or dark gray = person in mourning
- Bleached white = political candidate
- Purple toga with gold embroidery = victorious general
- All-purple toga = emperor

## Making (and Keeping) White Clothes White

In ancient times, pure white clothing was a sign of purity and high status. But keeping clothes white in the midst of dirt roads and dusty villages wasn't easy. One way ancient garment makers and clothes cleaners whitened fabric was by washing and soaking it in old urine. Yep. Urine. Pee. It turns out the ammonia in urine is an amazing bleaching agent. Bet you didn't know that! Urine was collected and even bought and sold for this purpose.

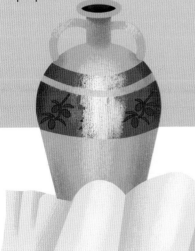

## Bugs, Snails, and Color

Purple dye was produced from the mucous gland of a sea snail called hexaplex trunculus.

Scarlet dye came from a tiny scaled insect called kermes echinatus that lived on oak trees.

Crimson and purple were royal colors because they cost so much to make and there were no substitutes.

Fishing on the Sea of Galilee supported a huge food export industry. Without refrigeration, fresh fish goes bad pretty fast. To make it last, and make it portable, people preserved fish in a spicy, salty pickling sauce and sent it all over the Roman Empire. The town of Magdala was a sardine-pickling center. Jesus' friend Mary Magdalene was probably from Magdala.

FISH SAUCE

Builders worked with wood and stone to make buildings, furniture, boats, carts, and anything that required skill and tools. Jesus' father, Joseph, was described as a carpenter.

# THE WORKING LIFE

The people who worked in ancient Palestine worked hard. Most labored as farmers, but worked land owned by others. About ninety percent of the people were directly involved in some form of agriculture—farming various crops, fishing in the Sea of Galilee, and herding sheep and goats. Other workers did manual labor, like carrying things or assisting skilled workers called artisans. This smaller class of people had specialized skills, like pottery or stone cutting. Artisans sometimes worked for themselves and sold their goods or labor.

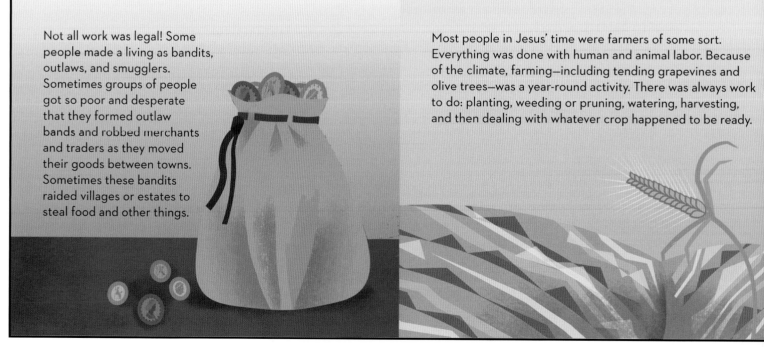

Not all work was legal! Some people made a living as bandits, outlaws, and smugglers. Sometimes groups of people got so poor and desperate that they formed outlaw bands and robbed merchants and traders as they moved their goods between towns. Sometimes these bandits raided villages or estates to steal food and other things.

Most people in Jesus' time were farmers of some sort. Everything was done with human and animal labor. Because of the climate, farming—including tending grapevines and olive trees—was a year-round activity. There was always work to do: planting, weeding or pruning, watering, harvesting, and then dealing with whatever crop happened to be ready.

Stonecutters and masons used iron tools to shape and carve the most common building material in the land. The big temple project in Jerusalem employed skilled stone workers (maybe as many as 18,000!) and used local hard limestone.

Weavers turned wool and linen thread into fabric for clothing. Others worked with dyes, making the woven fabric colorful.

Potters and basket weavers made cooking and carrying containers from clay and reeds.

Herding grazing animals was a common way to make a living in Jesus' time—and for centuries before that. The rocky, hilly landscape worked well for animals like sheep and goats, which needed someone to keep track of them. Large flocks owned by wealthy landowners were tended by hired shepherds. Nomadic Bedouin families kept their own flocks. By the time of Jesus, shepherds were looked down upon as being unskilled and suspicious.

References to sheep (including lambs, rams, and ewes) show up in the Bible more than five hundred times.

Fishing was a major part of life in Galilee. Bethsaida, where Jesus spent much of his time, was a big fishing center.

# FISHING ON THE SEA OF GALILEE

The Sea of Galilee is the largest freshwater lake in this region. The lake gets its water from underground springs and the Jordan River, which starts north of the lake in the Hula Valley. People have likely been catching and eating fish from this body of water for more than ten thousand years! In Jesus' time, one report suggested there were more than two hundred boats actively fishing on the lake.

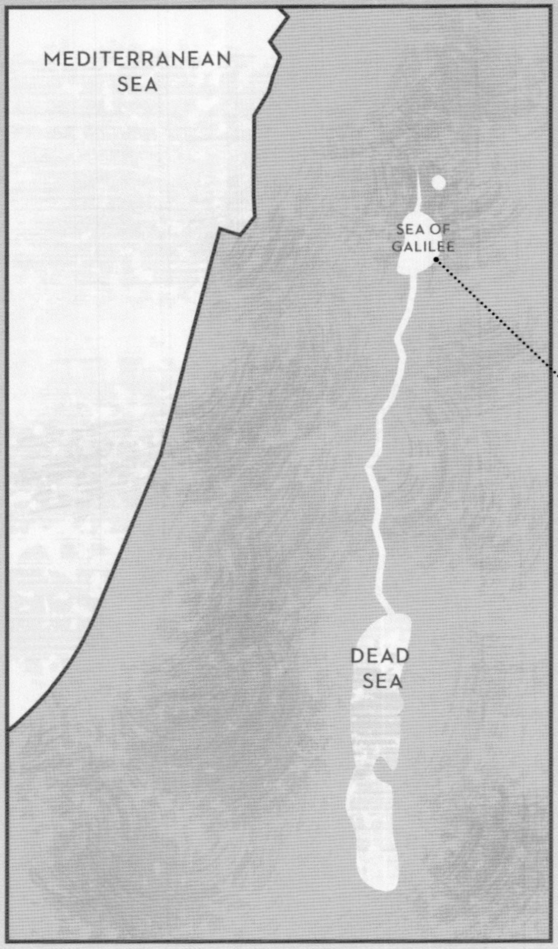

With such simple rigging, fishing boats were hard to sail if the lake got too rough.

Also called:
- the Sea of Tiberias
- the Lake of Kinneret
- the Lake of Genessaret

Because they had to get in and out of the water a lot, fishermen often worked naked. Fishing boats stayed close to shore, where they threw their nets, or dragged them along the bottom.

Boats were made of wood, and patched with whatever wood was available as they developed cracks and holes. The boats were small and not very stable. Each twenty-five-foot-long boat could hold four or five fishermen.

MEDITERRANEAN SEA

SEA OF GALILEE

DEAD SEA

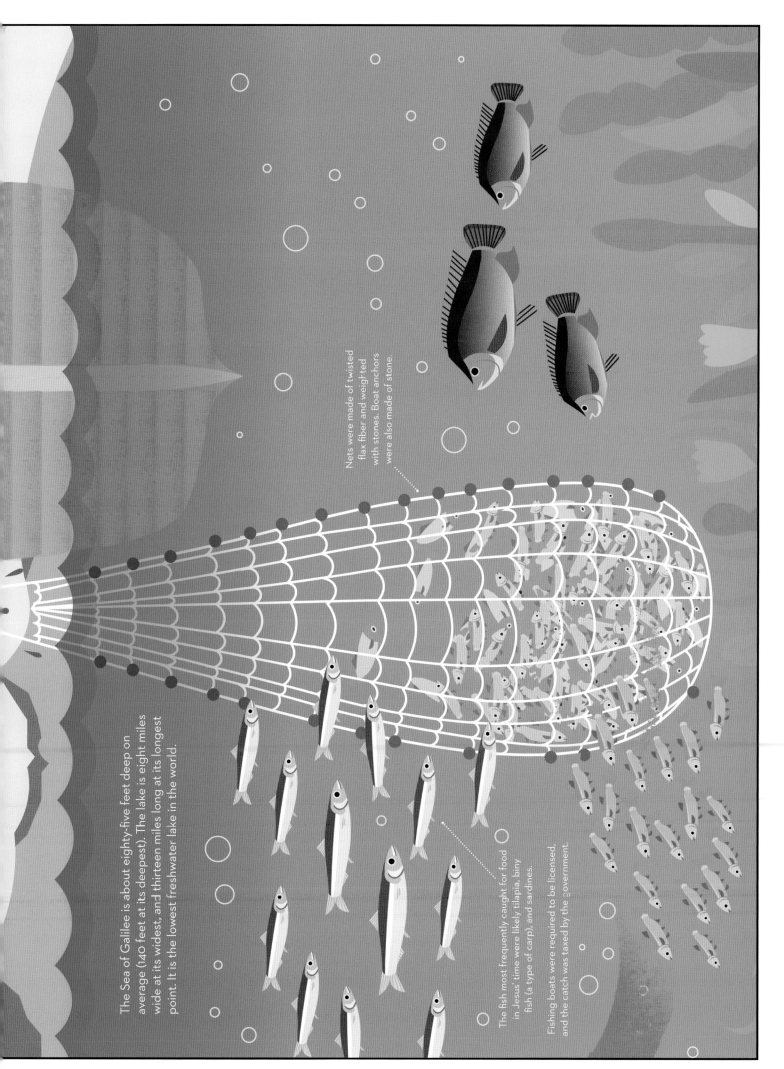

The Sea of Galilee is about eighty-five feet deep on average (140 feet at its deepest). The lake is eight miles wide at its widest, and thirteen miles long at its longest point. It is the lowest freshwater lake in the world.

Nets were made of twisted flax fiber and weighted with stones. Boat anchors were also made of stone.

The fish most frequently caught for food in Jesus' time were likely tilapia, biny fish (a type of carp), and sardines.

Fishing boats were required to be licensed, and the catch was taxed by the government.

# THE VINEYARD

A vineyard is a yard. With vines. It's both the place where grapevines grow and the place where the initial steps of making wine happen. In the first century, a vineyard would have a stone wall or hedge, or sometimes a ditch, defining its border and helping to keep out hungry goats, wild animals, and other grape thieves.

In addition to a wall, vineyards would have a watchtower, from which a guard would keep an eye on the valuable and delicious grapes as they grew ripe and juicy. Large vineyards would also have their own wine press cut into the limestone bedrock. Farmers with smaller vineyards would bring their ripe grapes to communal presses for processing.

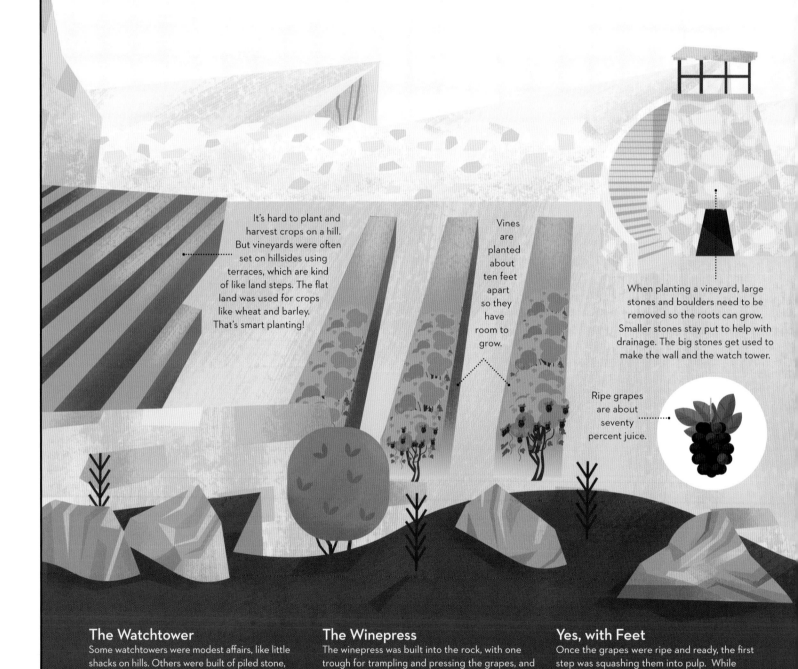

It's hard to plant and harvest crops on a hill. But vineyards were often set on hillsides using terraces, which are kind of like land steps. The flat land was used for crops like wheat and barley. That's smart planting!

Vines are planted about ten feet apart so they have room to grow.

When planting a vineyard, large stones and boulders need to be removed so the roots can grow. Smaller stones stay put to help with drainage. The big stones get used to make the wall and the watch tower.

Ripe grapes are about seventy percent juice.

### The Watchtower
Some watchtowers were modest affairs, like little shacks on hills. Others were built of piled stone, and were as tall as forty feet. In late summer, as the grapes were nearly ripe, the watchman would live in the tower, sometimes with his whole family. During the cold months, watchtowers would be abandoned.

### The Winepress
The winepress was built into the rock, with one trough for trampling and pressing the grapes, and lower vats to collect the pressed juice. Palestine's chalky limestone can be cut and carved more easily than harder stone, and holds liquid well.

### Yes, with Feet
Once the grapes were ripe and ready, the first step was squashing them into pulp. While different winemakers have used all sorts of tools for this part of the process, the people of the first century used their bare feet. Yep. In a land where most people wore sandals all the time. And remember, it was cleaner and safer than the water.

Wine-making, or **viticulture**, was a huge part of town life and village economy in Jesus' time. The hilly, rocky, limestone land and Mediterranean climate made much of Palestine a great place to grow grapes.

Which was a good thing, because water was a precious commodity in ancient Palestine. Towns and villages were often located near wells or, more rarely, natural springs. People hauled water from wells, and collected and stored rainwater in cisterns that were carved out of stone. Moving water was a heavy chore, requiring stone or clay jars and many, many trips between the community well and home. On top of all that work, stored water, as well as water collected from rivers and streams, was often contaminated and not safe to drink.

This is why wine was so important in the ancient world. The process of turning grape juice into alcoholic wine is called **fermentation**, and it makes the juice/wine safe-ish for drinking.

A back up vat, in case we need it.

A channel allows juice to run into a stone vat.

Clay jars were used to store wine and olive oil. Ancient Roman wine jars would hold about seven-and-a-half gallons. Jars were sealed with unfired clay or wax.

- Grapes grow in bunches. They actually belong to the berry family.

- Grapevines aren't grown by planting seeds. They are cultivated by planting cuttings or **slips** from other vines.

- New wine ferments in the vat for about three days. When the bubbling stops, it's time to take out the wine and put it into stone jars or other containers.

- **Fermentation** is a chemical process that uses yeasts (natural microorganisms) to convert sugars into heat and ethyl alcohol. Yeast loves to eat sugar. The grape skins contain natural yeasts which help start fermentation. Heat and alcohol are by-products, kind of like poop and sweat.

## The Harvest

Grape harvesting and wine-making was cause for celebration in ancient Palestine—obviously. Grapes were ready for harvest in late August and September, as the weather began to cool from the summer heat. This also happened to be about the same time as the Jewish festival of the new year, **Rosh Hashana**. The grape harvest was followed by the fig, olive, and tree fruit harvests, which ended with **Sukkoth**, the outdoor festival of booths, which is kind of what it sounds like—people setting up huts to share their bounty with others.

Being a vineyard owner meant you had a pretty good life. It takes a few years for newly cultivated grapevines to produce fruit mature enough for wine-making. If you're worried about where your next meal is coming from, or having to move all the time because of war or other upheaval, carving a wine press out of your hillside and waiting on grapevines is not the first thing on your mind. So winemakers tended to be pretty well-off and settled in.

# AGRICULTURE

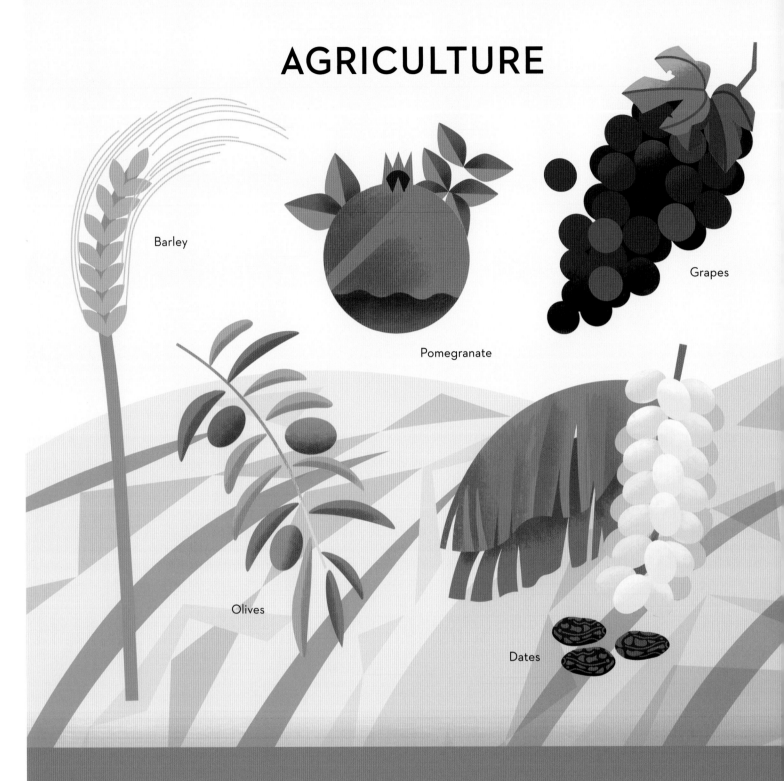

Barley

Pomegranate

Grapes

Olives

Dates

"For the Lord your God is bringing you into a good land, a land with flowing streams, with springs and underground waters welling up in valleys and hills, a land of wheat and barley, of vines and fig trees and pomegranates, a land of olive trees and honey, a land where you may eat bread without scarcity, where you will lack nothing, a land whose stones are iron and from whose hills you may mine copper." Deuteronomy 8:7-9

The seven fruits of the land referred to in the book of Deuteronomy are known as the "seven species." God promised the people, as they headed into Canaan, that they'd find good land, with water and enough food for them to not only survive but prosper. They did, and most of the farmable land was dedicated to these seven crops. With them, the Hebrew people could make everything they needed.

The grains, like barley and wheat, were used to make bread and porridge. Grapes were eaten fresh, and also became wine. Olives provided oil. Figs and dates were eaten as fruit and also used to make a kind of sweet syrup, which is likely what

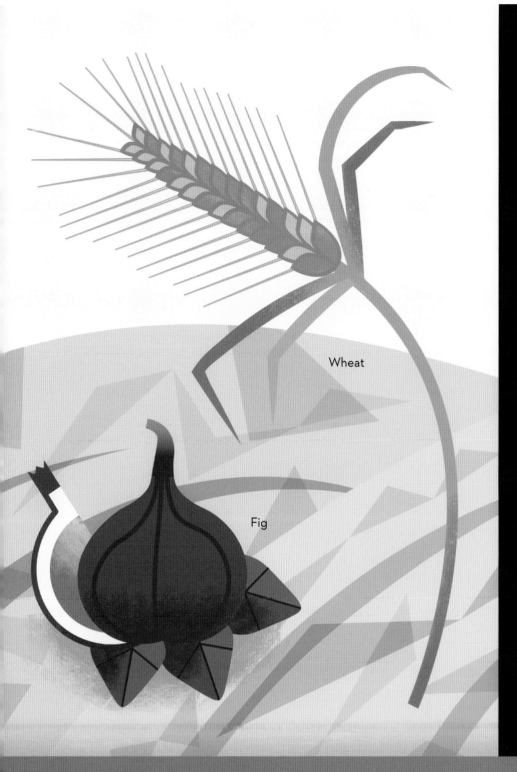

Wheat

Fig

## A Land of Milk and Honey

God famously described the land of Canaan as so rich a place that it flowed with milk and honey. It makes for a delicious, if sticky, vision of happiness. Bee honey, from wild sources, would have been fairly common in Jesus' time, as would the syrup made from dates that grew along the Jordan River. Because milk doesn't stay fresh for long outside the fridge—and Jesus didn't have a fridge—most milk, be it from cows, goats, sheep, or camels, was pretty quickly curdled into a kind of cheesy yogurt that you could slurp or eat with a spoon. So milk and honey as we know them might not be exactly what people found in the Promised Land, but "the Land of Camel Curds and Date Goo" doesn't quite have the same catchy ring.

## Light on the Veggies

Jesus and his friends probably didn't eat many salads. Vegetables like carrots, potatoes, and lettuce aren't mentioned in the Bible, and wouldn't have been part of the crop plans of first-century farmers. Onions, leeks, melons, cucumbers, and garlic were grown in the warm, marshy areas of the Nile delta down in Egypt. But the higher, dryer, and cooler elevations of most of the Palestinian farmland was better suited to olives and grapes.

One of the Bible's many rules about how to behave during harvest time says that you can enjoy a couple handfuls of grapes while you're walking in your neighbor's vineyard, but don't fill up a basket (Deuteronomy 23:24).

Deuteronomy refers to as honey. Along with being key ingredients of the ancient diet of those who lived in the land, these seven foods have been important as symbols for centuries.

The land and the landscape provided a decent climate for farming as well as raising animals. Sheep and goats were raised for milk, meat, wool, and leather. Cows gave milk and supplied the occasional feast. People kept chickens and roosters, which provided eggs, meat, and alarm clocks. Pigeons and doves were also domesticated and raised for meat. The Sea of Galilee contained schools of fish, which were caught in nets and eaten fresh, or salted and dried using salt from the Mediterranean or the Dead Sea.

Without access to supermarkets, truck and railroad transportation of food, or modern conveniences like refrigeration, tractors, and plastic, making sure your family had enough to eat from day to day and year to year was everybody's full-time job. Ancient people ate what they could grow, find, or catch. Often they traded what they had lots of for what they needed.

# OLIVES AND THEIR AMAZING OIL

- Along with wheat and grapes, olives were the most valuable product in Palestinian agriculture. While some olives were eaten as fruit, most got turned into oil, which could be stored, shipped, and sold.

- Olive trees are some of the heartiest and most resilient trees in the world. They're able to tolerate most soil types, handle even salty water, keep their leaves year-round, and produce fruit for hundreds of years.

- Olives were harvested in the fall, before the first rains.

- In this region, olive trees grow everywhere from southern Judea to northern Galilee.

- A mature olive tree can produce up to fifteen gallons of oil each year.

- Olive wood was valued by carpenters. It is very hard and resists rot.

- On what is now known as Palm Sunday, Jesus made his way into Jerusalem riding on a donkey. The people greeted him by waving palm branches, but it's likely some of them were waving olive branches taken from the orchards that can still be seen on the Mount of... wait for it...Olives.

- Olives are handpicked and collected in baskets, or shaken loose into nets or blankets by tree climbers. Occasionally, harvesters with long sticks or wooden rakes knock the olives out of the treetops.

Olive oil lamps were used to light dark homes. They were most often made of clay. Some were very elaborate.

Turning olives into oil is a multistep process. It starts with the olives being placed in a mill where they get smushed into a pulp, pits and all.

## The Olive Mill

The heavy grinding stone crushes the olives, pits and all, into a pulp. ............

The millstone is moved by people or donkey power. ............

The pulp is scooped into loosely woven baskets. ............

Some oil is collected during the grind. ............

Some oil drips out of the baskets and is collected. In Jesus' time, this pure oil got used in temple offerings as fuel oil for the menorah.

## The Olive Press

**First Press Oil** was used for the temple offering and as payments for goods and services. It was as good as gold. **Second Press Oil** was used for food, cosmetics, and medicine. **Third Press Oil** was used in oil lamps and made into soap.

Long, heavy beams usually made of oak.

Stacks of mesh baskets with pulp.

Pressed oil runs from the press into a storage vat, usually carved into the limestone.

- Most olive orchards were owned by wealthy landowners who had their own presses, and hired local people (or used their slaves) to do the work.

- Some villages had a community oil press which allowed people who had only a handful of trees to come on down and make oil.

- During the olive harvest, almost everybody in the community helped. The work had to be done quickly or the olives might spoil.

- Since the olive harvest happened late in the fall, this whole process was done indoors or in some kind of covered area to keep the oil from getting goopy (not a technical term).

- The pulp that was left over after all the pressings made a great fuel for ovens, stoves, and kilns.

# THE LIFE OF A WOMAN

Daily life for women in Jesus' time varied a bit depending on where they lived and how wealthy they were. Life in the cities was vastly different from day-to-day living in small villages and farming or fishing communities. But rich or poor, women kept the ancient household running. They were in charge of feeding, clothing, and cleaning up for the family.

Jewish women were also religious leaders at home. The mother of the house said table prayers and led the candle lighting during *Shabbat* (Sabbath) and other festivals. Children were taught to honor father *and* mother.

## Religion

At the time, the Jewish religion made several distinctions between women and men:

- Only men could be priests.
- Some parts of the temple were closed to women.
- A menstruating woman was considered impure. Jewish law said that anyone who came into contact with a woman while she was menstruating was also unclean, so women often stayed out of the public eye while they were having their periods.
- Women were also considered impure after giving birth to a baby. This impurity lasted seven days.

## Work

Like the men of the time, women most likely knew and worked closely with their neighbors. Women often worked alongside other men and women in agriculture jobs and the marketplace. Roman culture allowed women to conduct their own business, lend money, own slaves, study philosophy, and take jobs as nurses or teachers. It's not clear if rural and poor Jewish women had the same kind of freedom, but it's very likely that women were active beyond their homes and immediate neighborhoods.

A woman who lived to the ripe old age of 50 probably would have given birth to six children. Only two or three of these children would survive to be adults.

Women who were household slaves often cared for children or did housework. Agricultural slaves worked in fields, fabric dyeing operations, and fish processing areas.

Women were often married by the time they were fifteen.

## Home Life

In villages and towns, ordinary women shopped for, harvested, prepared, served, and cleaned up all meal-related stuff. And that was a lot of work. To provide food for her family, a woman would need to:

- Grind grain for flour. Make dough. Bake bread.
- Milk animals. Make cheese.
- Tend cooking fires.
- Harvest garden produce.
- Purchase or trade at market for food.
- Serve a breakfast of small amounts of food—sometimes it was yesterday's leftovers plus today's bread—that family members took with them to work.
- Prepare the main meal: a stew with some kind of meat or fish, salt, onions, coriander, mint, or dill. Serve bread, cheese, wine, and fruit. Use the bread for dipping.
- Get ready to do it all again tomorrow.

Wealthy people had slaves to do these things. The slaves were usually women.

## Economics

The Jewish, Greek, and Roman cultures were **patriarchal**, which means "father rule" in Greek. This meant, among other things, that men made the rules, and women were seen as dependent on male strength, intelligence, morality, and control. In this system, daughters were a liability and widows were vulnerable.

But women didn't always go along with this. There were female business owners, and women who took care of themselves and their families without men. Of course, this was easier for women with money. But poor women without husbands didn't have many options. That's why Jesus often spoke about the importance of taking care of widows and orphans. They were some of the most vulnerable people in the culture.

The early Christian movement was known for the way it allowed women to have positions of honor, prominence, and leadership.

Women helped arrange marriages for their children.

Roman and Jewish girls and women were expected to be modest, work hard, and follow the rules of their families and cultures.

41

# THE JEWISH CALENDAR

The Jewish year isn't a line with a start and a finish. It's a circle that follows the circle of the seasons. People who farm and keep herds of animals are tuned in to the changes in the weather and land. In Jesus' day, they kept time by what the weather was like and what work needed to be done.

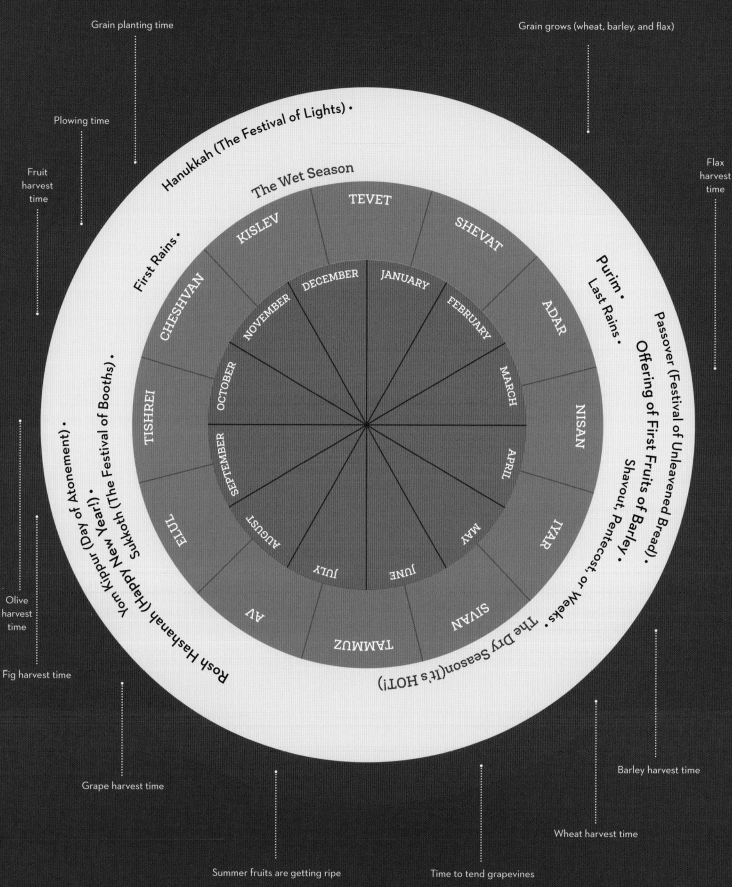

Grain planting time

Grain grows (wheat, barley, and flax)

Plowing time

Flax harvest time

Fruit harvest time

Hanukkah (The Festival of Lights) •

The Wet Season

TEVET

First Rains •

KISLEV

SHEVAT

Purim •
Last Rains •

CHESHVAN

DECEMBER

JANUARY

FEBRUARY

ADAR

NOVEMBER

Passover (Festival of Unleavened Bread) •
Offering of First Fruits of Barley •
Shavout, Pentecost, or Weeks • The Dry Season (it's HOT!)

TISHREI

OCTOBER

MARCH

NISAN

Yom Kippur (Day of Atonement) •
Sukkkoth (The Festival of Booths) •

SEPTEMBER

APRIL

Olive harvest time

ELUL

IYAR

Rosh Hashanah (Happy New Year!) •

AUGUST

MAY

Fig harvest time

AV

JULY

JUNE

SIVAN

TAMMUZ

Barley harvest time

Grape harvest time

Wheat harvest time

Summer fruits are getting ripe

Time to tend grapevines

## Festivals and the Land

You may notice that the festivals in the big circle happen around the same times as certain activities of harvest or planting. This is no accident. The ancient Jewish religious festivals fit into and celebrated the life and productivity of the land that God gave the people.

The new year begins as the rich fruits are getting ripe and ready to enjoy. Rosh Hashanah is also wine-making time! The Jewish New Year is a time of feasting and celebration for the good gifts of God.

The Hebrew month names come from Babylonian words. They were adopted by the Jews while they lived in exile there, starting almost six hundred years before Jesus.

 Planting season

 Jewish festivals and holy days

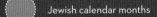 Jewish calendar months

 Roman calendar months

## The Calendar and the Moon

Unlike the Roman calendar we use today, which is a solar calendar, and tracks the earth's revolution around the sun for timekeeping, the Jewish calendar is lunar. It measures each month by the cycle of the moon. Because moon cycles don't quite add up to a thirty- or thirty-one-day month (they're closer to twenty-seven or twenty-eight), every three years or so, they add an extra month! The month added is a second "Adar," which happens in the spring. The year with the extra month is called a "pregnant year."

In the time of Jesus, the Sanhedrin was responsible for deciding when to add an extra Adar. Their goal was to make sure the festival of Passover always happened in the spring, at more or less the same time.

# THE GREAT SANHEDRIN

The Great, or Jerusalem, Sanhedrin was an assembly of seventy Jewish elders—plus the High Priest—who were the highest religious and governing authority among the Jewish people. This was the group that discussed and settled religious questions and passed judgment on those who broke Torah law. They were the "Supreme Court" of ancient Israel.

The seventy members of the Sanhedrin were required to be serious, wise, knowledgeable about everything, good-looking, not disabled, at least forty years old, from priestly families, and male. Members of the Sanhedrin came from the more wealthy or elite class.

The Sanhedrin supervised the temple services and priestly activities. They also controlled the temple treasury.

The Great Sanhedrin was the only authority that could:

- Put a Jewish king on trial
- Extend the boundaries of Jerusalem and the temple
- Settle questions about Torah interpretation

During Jesus' time, the Sanhedrin was not allowed to pass a sentence of death. That right belonged to the Roman authorities.

Each city in the land had a Sanhedrin, though most were smaller (usually twenty-three members), and they met to decide local matters. These were called Lesser Sanhedrins.

*San-HEE-drin* means "sitting together." It's a Hebrew version of a Greek word.

What about the Roman government? Well, authority isn't always authority. The Roman rulers of ancient Palestine were mostly interested in maintaining control and collecting taxes. They were happy to allow local Jewish leaders to settle internal arguments and keep things peaceful.

The very first Sanhedrin, ordered by God, included Moses as the High Priest (see Numbers 11:16).

The Sadducees and Pharisees often battled each other for influence and control.

Rabbis
Aristocrats
Priests
Sadducees
Pharisees

The chief of the Sanhedrin was called the *Rosh HaYeshiva* or "Head of the Sitting."

The group sat in a semi-circle so that everybody could see everybody else. The United States' founders borrowed the ancient Sanhedrin's layout for the Senate!

The Jerusalem Sanhedrin met in a room cut into the north wall of the temple (the temple walls were very thick!) called The Chamber of Cut Stones. The room had a door that led into the temple and a door that led outside. They met to discuss matters every day except during religious festivals and on the Sabbath.

The Sanhedrin wasn't allowed to enter a final judgment on a matter unless everybody was present.

# THE JERUSALEM TEMPLE

## The Holiest Place
According to the Jews, God lived here. Nobody but the High Priest entered this small room, and then only once a year (on Yom Kippur) to ask forgiveness for the whole nation. Called The Holy of Holies, this room was *totally empty*.

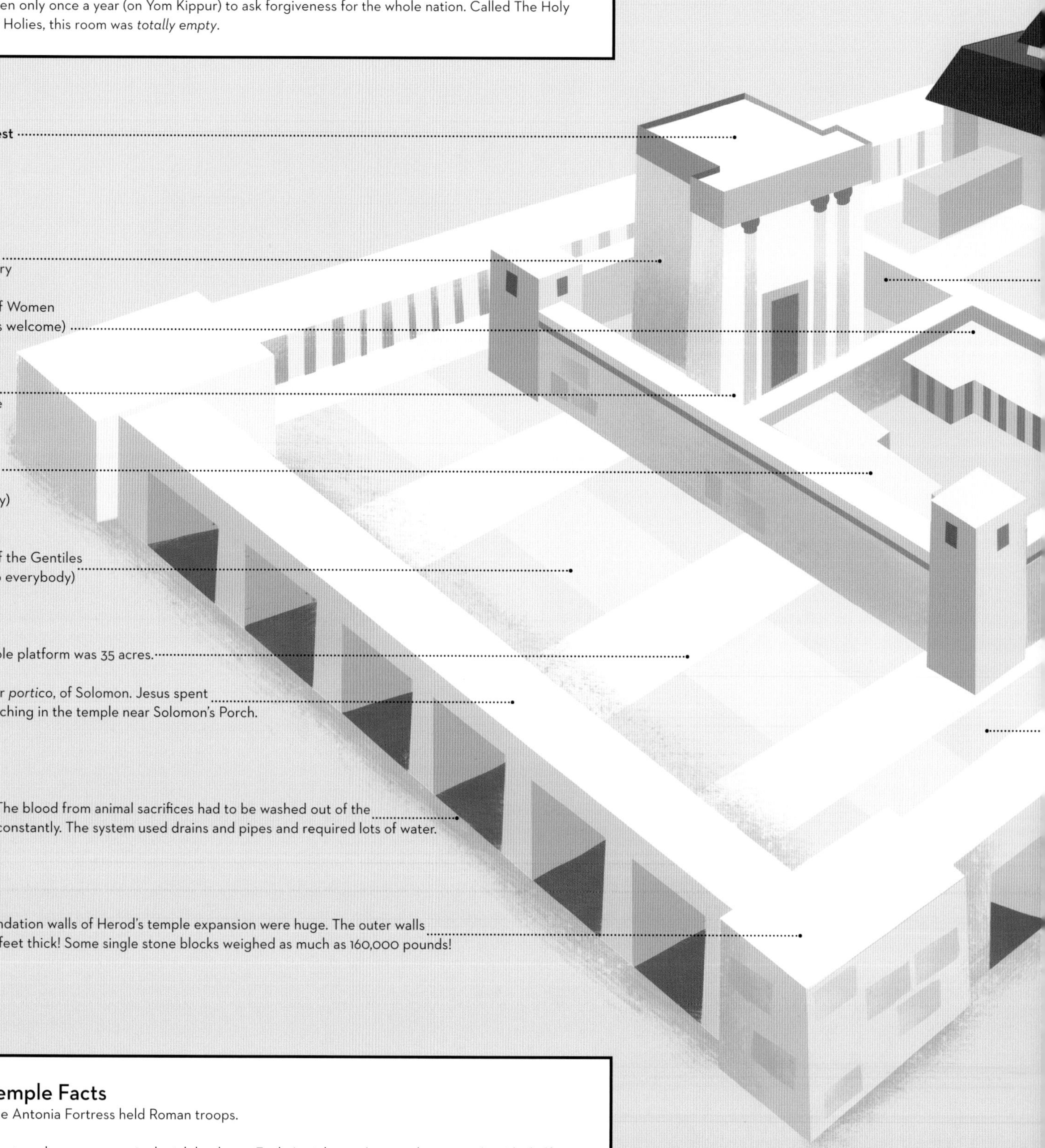

***Holiest

Central
Sanctuary

Court of Women
(all Jews welcome)
*holy

Altar of
Sacrifice

Court
of Israel
(Jewish
men only)
**holier

Court of the Gentiles
(open to everybody)

The whole platform was 35 acres.

Porch, or *portico*, of Solomon. Jesus spent
time teaching in the temple near Solomon's Porch.

Drains. The blood from animal sacrifices had to be washed out of the
temple constantly. The system used drains and pipes and required lots of water.

The foundation walls of Herod's temple expansion were huge. The outer walls
were 16 feet thick! Some single stone blocks weighed as much as 160,000 pounds!

## Temple Facts
The Antonia Fortress held Roman troops.

The temple was an amazingly rich bank too. Each Jewish man (age twelve or over) paid a half-shekel temple tax every year.

Because there were parts of the temple where only priests were allowed, Herod had one thousand priests trained as stonemasons and builders for the renovation.

Pilgrims went barefoot in the temple.

Because, obviously, there are no photos of the temple, and architectural drawings weren't a thing in the first century, we don't really have a clear image of what the great temple of Jerusalem looked like. We do have written descriptions and ruins, which help modern-day wonderers make good guesses. So we know that the temple was: important, impressive, and utterly destroyed.

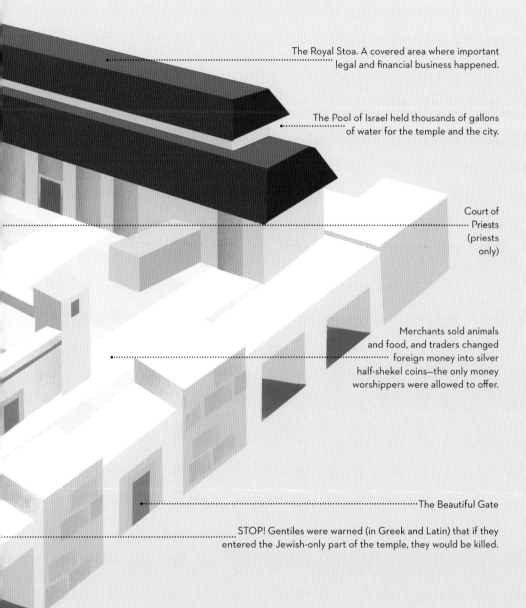

The Royal Stoa. A covered area where important legal and financial business happened.

The Pool of Israel held thousands of gallons of water for the temple and the city.

Court of Priests (priests only)

Merchants sold animals and food, and traders changed foreign money into silver half-shekel coins—the only money worshippers were allowed to offer.

The Beautiful Gate

STOP! Gentiles were warned (in Greek and Latin) that if they entered the Jewish-only part of the temple, they would be killed.

## The Temple Timeline

**70 CE:**
The temple is totally destroyed by the Romans.

**37 BCE:**
Herod the Great, de facto king of the region, undertakes a major renovation and expansion of the temple so that the Jewish people will accept him as their ruler. The work takes eighty years to finish.

**507 BCE:**
The temple is rebuilt with permission from the ruling Persians.

**587 BCE:**
The Babylonians destroy the temple.

**1000 BCE:**
King Solomon builds the first temple.

## Sacrifices

The temple was the center of Jewish religion. Faithful Jews made pilgrimages from Judea, Galilee, and all over the empire to the temple three times a year. Priests in the temple helped the nation stay right with God by constantly offering sacrifices.

Following the Torah's instructions, faithful Jews brought offerings of money, grain, oil, and flour as well as animals, which were sacrificed by the priests.

- Wealthy people could afford to sacrifice an ox.
- Less wealthy families would bring a lamb.
- Poor people offered pigeons.

Sometimes the whole animal was burned; sometimes parts of the animal were burned (for God) and the rest eaten by the priests or by the person who had brought the animal as an offering. Priests splashed the blood of animal offerings on the Altar of Sacrifice.

# THE BIBLE* JESUS KNEW

*The word *Bible* comes from Latin and Greek words for "book." But Jesus and other people of his time didn't use books with covers and bindings and pages. The Jewish scriptures, like many ancient documents between the eras of clay tablets and folder-style books, were written out on scrolls. By the way, **scripture** is what we call a religion's sacred writings, usually considered inspired by God.

## GENESIS, EXODUS, LEVITICUS, NUMBERS, DEUTERONOMY

The **Torah,** also known as the Teaching, the Law, the Books of Moses, and the *Pentateuch* (Greek for "Five Scrolls"), was the central scripture for all Jews. It consists of what Christians consider the first five books of the Old Testament. These books tell the story of God's ongoing faithfulness to the Jewish people. They also contain God's laws for how to live, how to worship, and how to be in relationship with God.

In ancient Palestine, every Jewish community would have a copy of the Torah scrolls. They would read from the Torah every Sabbath and at every religious festival. Like most faithful Jewish men, Jesus knew the Torah well. He studied and discussed it from an early age.

## PROPHETS

Many Jews of Jesus' time also read and studied books written by and about Hebrew prophets. Some of these are part of our Bible, but others are lost forever. The prophets were women and men who, throughout the Israelites' history, spoke God's words of judgment and comfort to the people. Jesus seems to have considered the prophets' writings part of Jewish scripture. He often quoted from the book of Isaiah—one of these prophets—and sometimes referred to "The Law and the Prophets" when he spoke.

### Reading
The Torah was intended to be read out loud in public, and then explained and discussed.

The Torah was the only scripture accepted by the Sadducees.

Jesus quotes from Deuteronomy more than any other book (see Deuteronomy 6:5 and then Matthew 22:37, for example).

Readers stood to read, and hearers stood to hear.

It's likely that many synagogue services also included readings from the prophets and the writings.

See Luke 4:16-30 for a story about synagogue reading in Jesus' time. Jesus read from the scroll of Isaiah, and then mentioned stories from the book of Kings. The people listening weren't fans of his teaching—they tried to throw him off a cliff!

Jesus may have been familiar with a Greek version of Hebrew scripture that was written by rabbis in Alexandria, Egypt, starting 300 years before he was born.

Scrolls were often made of animal skin that was soaked, scraped, and stretched into thin, long-lasting parchment. Usually the skin was from a calf, sheep, or goat. Ancient Babylonian and Syrian Torah scrolls were sometimes made from deerskin parchment. Other scrolls were made from **papyrus**, a kind of paper made from plants.

## WRITINGS

In addition to the five books of the Torah and books written by the prophets, first-century Jewish people would have known and loved a handful of other writings that were a deep part of their religious tradition and were already ancient even then:

- Psalms: Songs, prayers, and poems of lament, celebration, and worship
- Proverbs: Wisdom sayings
- The Song of Solomon: Love poetry
- Stories about heroes and heroines, like Ruth, Job, Esther, Daniel, and Israel's kings

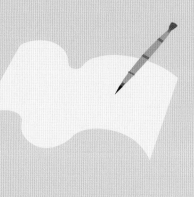

### Writing
Torah scrolls were copied by hand and written in Hebrew, which is read from right to left. It's possible that some scrolls in Jesus' time also included writing in Greek or Aramaic.

Each Torah scroll contains almost 305,000 individual letters.

It takes almost a whole year (working six hours a day) to copy an entire Torah scroll.

Scribes copied scrolls using reeds sharpened into writing instruments. They were often well-respected scholars. Writing was a rare and valuable skill.

First-century Jewish scholars and rabbis argued about what counted as official scripture. Everyone agreed on the Torah. The final canon (official list) wasn't firmed up for another 100 years.

# CRUCI-FIXION
### (cross)       (attaching)

## OFFICIALLY, A REALLY BAD WAY TO DIE

Under Roman law, robbers, army deserters, traitors, and rebels could be crucified. Jesus was crucified for rebelling against the Roman government. Slave owners were also allowed to crucify rebellious or disobedient slaves. Condemned criminals were tied or nailed to wooden crosses in public places, where people would watch them slowly die. Crucified people usually died by suffocation, as their cramped thorax muscles made it impossible for them to breathe.

Crucifixion was intended to be:
- Painful
- Terrifying
- Humiliating

Crucifixion of criminals was not a Roman invention. Other ancient cultures, including the Jews, practiced similar methods of public execution. The Jews of Jesus' time referred to crucifixion as "hanging on a tree."

## OTHER METHODS OF EXECUTING CRIMINALS

**Stoning:** This was a biblically approved method of killing a criminal—it was the go-to punishment for sins against God. Stoning involved a group of people throwing rocks at a person until that person died. That way, no one person was responsible for the death. This was generally a very slow way to die.

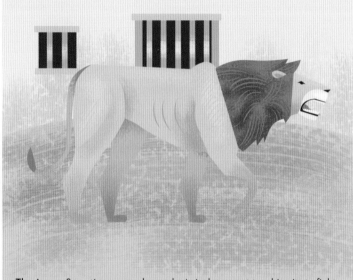

**The Arena:** Sometimes a condemned criminal was sent to a big city to fight as a gladiator in the public games. Gladiators were usually killed by other gladiators or by wild animals.

**Burning:** Like crucifixion, public burning was a dramatic warning to other potential criminals.

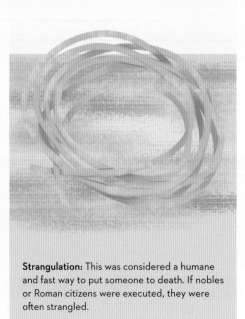

**Strangulation:** This was considered a humane and fast way to put someone to death. If nobles or Roman citizens were executed, they were often strangled.

**Decapitation:** Cutting off someone's head was quick, and the head could be displayed as a warning to others. It was often a show of domination and victory over an enemy. John the Baptist was beheaded.

A sign, called a **titulus**, told passersby what the crime was. The sign on Jesus' cross was an acronym for the Latin version of "Jesus of Nazareth, the King of the Jews"

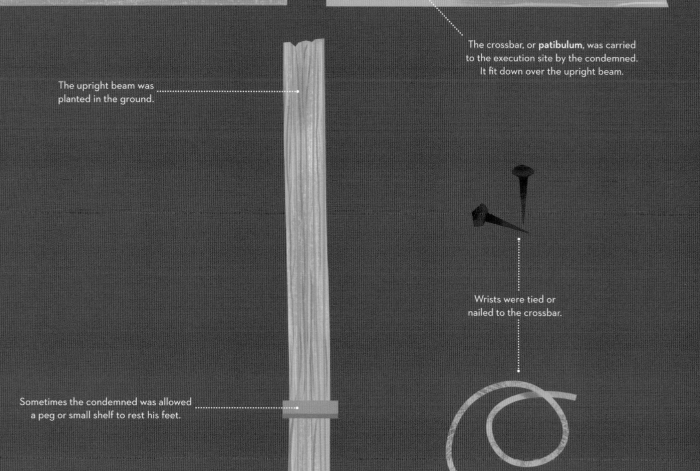

The crossbar, or **patibulum**, was carried to the execution site by the condemned. It fit down over the upright beam.

The upright beam was planted in the ground.

Wrists were tied or nailed to the crossbar.

Sometimes the condemned was allowed a peg or small shelf to rest his feet.

On a low cross, the condemned person's feet hung about eighteen inches from the ground.

## DIFFERENT TYPES OF CROSSES ALL HAD THE SAME EFFECT.

| Crux Simplex | Crux Commissa | Crux Decussata | Crux Immissa | Inverted Cross |
|---|---|---|---|---|

# DEATH AND BURIAL

Death was a daily reality in the ancient world. Rich people and poor people alike got sick and died, and somebody had to take care of their bodies. Usually, a person's family tended to their remains, but people without families nearby, such as soldiers far from home, joined burial societies so someone would be available to give them a decent burial. The details of death and burial varied based on a person's ethnic and religious traditions.

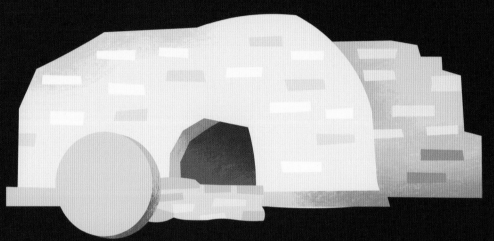

### The Jewish Way

Jewish people buried their dead. Tombs around Jerusalem were carved into the limestone cliffs and small entry doors were sealed with square stone "plugs" or covered by round slabs of stone that could be rolled away. This is how Jesus was buried.

Poor people were buried in shallow pits wrapped in cloth. Jews didn't use coffins or do any kind of embalming to help preserve the body. Instead, bodies were wrapped in strips of cloth or **shrouds**—a kind of linen covering. Funerals and burials were supposed to happen within one day of death, but no funerals were allowed on the Sabbath.

In Judaism, giving a decent burial to a stranger is considered a good deed, just like feeding the hungry and clothing the naked.

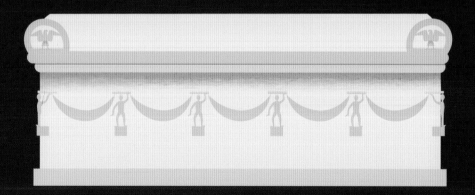

### The Greek and Egyptian Way

Other people in this part of the world practiced **embalming**—preserving—the dead with salt or herbs. Egyptians were famous for carefully preparing their dead nobility for the next life. Greeks and Egyptians were big fans of carved and decorated **sarcophagi**, which are stone coffins. (The singular form is **sarcophagus**.) Burial practices for the wealthy involved elaborate funerals, and people were often buried with clothing, food, and tools because it was believed they could use them in the afterlife. As you may have guessed by now, poor people were usually wrapped in simple cloth and buried in shallow holes or pits.

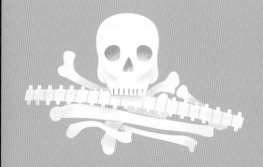

- Wealthy families had family tombs, which allowed generations to stay together after death. After a body had lain for a year on a shelf in the tomb, family members gathered up the bones and stacked them carefully in a stone box called an **ossuary**. This helped make room in family tombs for more bodies. Carved from stone, ossuaries were about two feet wide and fifteen inches deep.

  An area with many tombs was called a *necropolis*, which means "city of the dead" in Greek.

- The scriptures Jesus knew don't say much about the fate of the dead. God is the God of the living, and just as the dead are cut off from their living families, the Hebrew scriptures assume the dead are cut off from God as well. Most Jews believed that death was an ending, and that the dead would inhabit a slow, dim, sleepy place called Sheol. Ideas about afterlife and places where the dead continue to exist came into Jewish thought and belief from other cultures, including the Greeks, Romans, and Egyptians.

  The possibility of God bringing the dead back to life in some sort of lasting way was debated by the Jewish scholars of Jesus' time. The Pharisees believed in this kind of resurrection. The Sadducees didn't. Jesus was clearly on the side of the Pharisees.

## The Roman Way

In the first century, Romans practiced **cremation**, or burning of the dead. This ensured that no one messed with the body of the dead person. Ashes and other leftover burned bits were collected, soaked in wine, and placed in jars or boxes. These containers were often buried in the ground or stored in a **columbarium**—a place to keep urns. Robbing graves or disturbing bones was a high crime. Romans waited eight days between death and the funeral.

One huge fear among every Middle Eastern culture was being left unburied after death, and being eaten and scattered by wild animals and birds. An ancient Mesopotamian curse says, "May the earth not receive your corpses"!

# ILLNESS

Ancient people got sick and hurt just like modern-day people do. But they understood the causes—and cures—of illness very differently than we do today.

## FOUR ANCIENT PERSPECTIVES ON ILLNESS

These four basic points of view got blended and used in different ways by different people and groups in ancient Palestine.

### You have a God problem, and you need to make it right.

This was the basic Jewish understanding. Since God is the ultimate healer, the only way to be sick would be to be far away from God spiritually. So sickness was seen as a sign of a bad relationship with God. For the Jews, **repentance** (being sorry about what you've done wrong and turning back to God), forgiveness, and healing are all connected. This is why Jesus often talked about people being healed and forgiven.

### You have an evil spirit inside you. Let's get it out.

Ancient people didn't understand mental illness the way modern people do. So illnesses that weren't obvious problems with the body were believed to be caused by demons and bad spirits. Getting better required **exorcism**, a ritual intervention by someone who could chase, bribe, trick, lure, or command the bad spirit away from or out of the sick person. In the Gospel of Mark, Jesus is portrayed as a powerful exorcist.

### The gods are against you. We should try to make them happy.

The Roman religion recognized many gods and divine forces, including the elements of the earth, like wind, fire, and water. If you were sick, you could give offerings to these gods in the hopes of getting back on their good sides and getting healthy again.

### The elements of your body are out of whack. We can fix that.

The ancient Greek physician Hippocrates refused to believe in demons or gods when it came to health and sickness. He taught that health came from the right balance of heat and cold, rest and activity, good nutrition and modest living. Sound familiar?

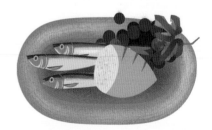

# MEDICINES

In Jesus' time, there were **faith healers** who used magic and religion to fix illness, and there were **physicians** who tried to help people heal by doing surgery, administering medicines, and prescribing procedures like bloodletting, sweating, and bathing in cold water. These healers used remedies including camel urine and porcupine blood to help heal wounds and cure heart pain.

- Olive oil was put on wounds to keep them soft and help with healing (Luke 10:34).

- Wine and honey have antiseptic (infection-fighting) properties.

- Saliva was thought to have healing qualities too (John 9:6).

# MAGIC

In the ancient world, magicians were more than entertainers. They claimed to provide mystical solutions for people's biggest problems. Folks in Jesus' time were very interested in magic, especially the idea that it might help them control the unpredictable parts of life, such as illness, bad weather, love, or the fate of enemies. Magicians made money by selling their services or making special charms and potions. They also would recite or write spells for a fee or a favor. We don't know if any of these charms or spells worked, but they certainly captured the imagination of people living in the first century.

## So, what does magic have to do with Jesus?

Potion

Magicians were not so popular with religious people. Hebrew scripture has no word for magic. It considers those who practice **sorcery** (using magic to control others) or **necromancy** (using magic to speak with the dead) to be evil.

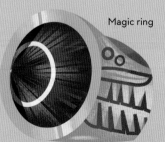

Bones

Ancient traditions link the Hebrew king, Solomon, who was famous for wisdom, with secret, magical knowledge.

Magicians looked for magic wherever they could find it. They added the names of powerful gods to their spells—even the Hebrew God!

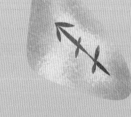

Magic stone with secret symbols and images, called **glyphs**

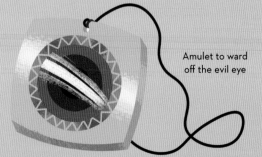

Amulet to ward off the evil eye

Because he performed miracles, some people accused Jesus of being a magician. They said that his power to heal came from Satan, or the demon Beelzebul (see Mark 3:20-35).

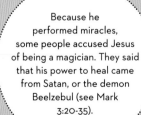

Magic ring

# MIRACLES

Miracles—the Bible also calls them signs or mighty works—demonstrate the power of God to accomplish amazing things without any other reasonable explanation. In the Hebrew Bible and Jewish tradition, miracles show divine might. These miracles often come about after a particularly holy person prays for them. Biblical miracle workers include Elisha and Elijah.

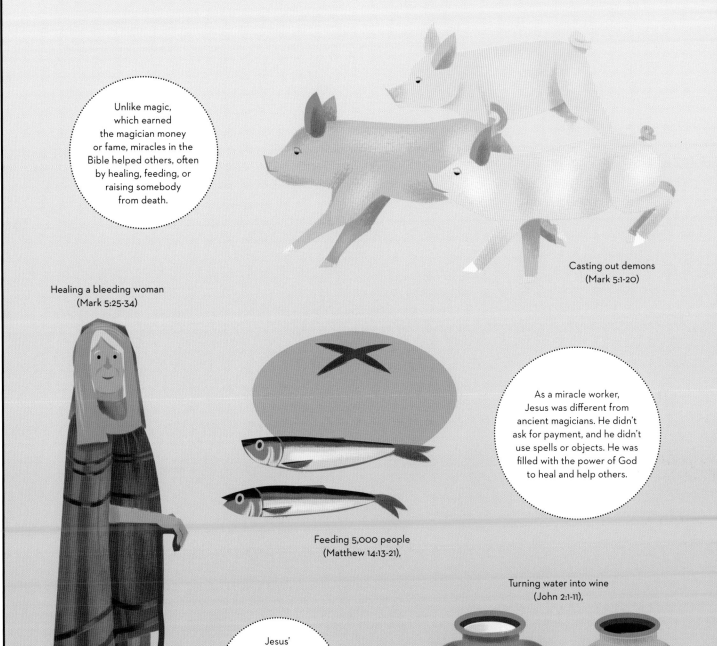

Unlike magic, which earned the magician money or fame, miracles in the Bible helped others, often by healing, feeding, or raising somebody from death.

Casting out demons
(Mark 5:1-20)

Healing a bleeding woman
(Mark 5:25-34)

As a miracle worker, Jesus was different from ancient magicians. He didn't ask for payment, and he didn't use spells or objects. He was filled with the power of God to heal and help others.

Feeding 5,000 people
(Matthew 14:13-21),

Turning water into wine
(John 2:1-11),

Jesus' followers saw healings like this one as an example of God's power working through Jesus.

# JESUS: HIS WORDS, HIS WORLD

Jesus was a real person who lived in a real place during a specific time in history. He ate food, wore clothes, walked on roads, slept, and experienced life.

When you read or hear stories about Jesus and his disciples and the crowds of people they met, think about everything you've discovered in this book. Now you know a bit about what their lives might have looked like, and maybe even what they had for breakfast!

Knowing more about the world Jesus lived in obviously makes you a little smarter. But it also helps you start seeing what Jesus was up to when he told stories about sheep and mustard seeds and money. Jesus used these everyday objects to help his friends and others understand how God works. He showed them that following God is about paying attention to forgotten things, caring about the people others ignore, and flipping ideas about power and influence upside down. In his life, death, and resurrection, Jesus put real skin and spit and blood on ideas about God, showing the people—all people—who God is and what God does.

Barns and farms
(Luke 12:16-21)

Flowers and birds
(Matthew 6:25-31)

Slaves
(Matthew 18:21-35)

Wine
(Luke 5:37-38)

Builders, building
trades (Luke 6:47-49)

Day laborers
(Matthew 20:1-16)

Thieves
(Matthew 24:42-44)

Vineyards
(Mark 12:1-8)

Widows
and judges
(Luke 18:2-8)

Sowing seeds
(Mark 4:3-8; 14-20)

Fig trees
(Luke 13:6-9)

Much of Jesus' teaching happened through parables. Jesus and the rabbis of his day often taught people using stories that contained normal, everyday experiences, places, objects, and people. A lot of what you have read about in this book shows up in Jesus' parables.

Most of Jesus' parables show up in the first three books of the New Testament—Matthew, Mark, and Luke. These three books, along with one more, John, are called **the Gospels** and they all tell stories from Jesus' life. Since these books are about the same person, there's some overlap in the stories they tell. Luke has 24 parables, including 18 that appear nowhere else. Matthew has 23 parables, with 11 that can't be found in the other Gospels. Mark has 8, with 2 that are only found there. John doesn't include any of Jesus' parables.

So go ahead and see for yourself! Read and think about stories of Jesus as well as the stories Jesus told and the things he said. Keep reading! Keep exploring! Keep learning!

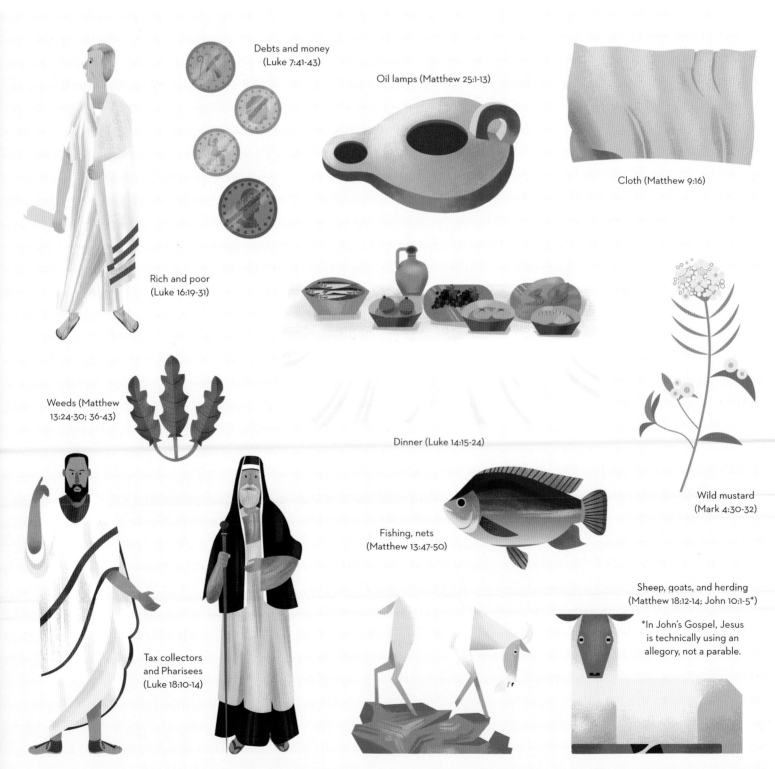

Debts and money
(Luke 7:41-43)

Oil lamps (Matthew 25:1-13)

Cloth (Matthew 9:16)

Rich and poor
(Luke 16:19-31)

Weeds (Matthew
13:24-30; 36-43)

Dinner (Luke 14:15-24)

Wild mustard
(Mark 4:30-32)

Fishing, nets
(Matthew 13:47-50)

Sheep, goats, and herding
(Matthew 18:12-14; John 10:1-5*)

Tax collectors
and Pharisees
(Luke 18:10-14)

*In John's Gospel, Jesus
is technically using an
allegory, not a parable.

# BIOS

**Marc Olson** is a theologian and a former pastor. He earned a Bachelor of Fine Arts from Pacific Lutheran University, and a Master of Divinity from Luther Seminary. He was also awarded the Seminary's International Preaching Fellowship in 2007, which resulted in a year abroad, studying and teaching with his family in Tanzania as well as Israel and Palestine. Marc lives in St Paul, Minnesota with his son, Sigurd, and their Basset Hound, Bruce. He also drives a garbage truck.

**Jemima Maybank** is an illustrator living in Leeds, England, who is fascinated by the ancient orthodox icons of saints found in many Cathedrals of the UK. In her free time she likes running and trying to stop her houseboat from sinking.